PRAISE FOR

WHAT MANNER OF MAN IS THIS?

"An insightful, informative piece and important addition to the literature of the development of The Bahamas.

The Islands of The Bahamas have served as the backdrop for any number of global game-changing events in the course of our history—European landfall in 1492, the extermination of a people, the enslavement of another, pirates and privateers, rum runners and drug smugglers. The arrival of the former King of England, Edward VIII, as Royal Governor of The Bahamas in 1940, was in keeping with the shady intrigue and scandalous behaviours sometimes associated with some residents and visitors to these shores.

Much has been written about the gallant former king, the Duke of Windsor, who gave up his throne for the love of a woman. Orville Turnquest has chosen as his subject the investigation of the character of the man who happened upon The Bahamas during a five year assignment as Royal Governor of the Bahama Islands beginning in 1940. This was a time when social and economic injustice against the majority black called out for enlightened leadership and action by those in authority. Turnquest found the Duke's leadership wanting at virtually every level. He assessed the Duke as weak, prejudiced, racist and disloyal.

Turnquest has produced an easy, readable history of the period, well-informed by his own personal experience as a young black, who overcame the absence of the opportunities gifted to the Duke of Windsor to become the Duke's successor in the office of governor general of an independent Bahamas.

This work will prove especially useful to students and to all those with an interest in the political development of a small island nation in the middle of the last century when the disadvantaged majority began to agitate for a sea change in the social mores, political leadership and economic opportunity."

THE RT. HON. HUBERT A. INGRAHAM
Former Prime Minister of The Bahamas

D1566706

"What a fascinating story! This comprehensive, thoroughly-researched masterpiece deserves its place as the history/geography/social sciences text of high schools and colleges and in libraries throughout The Bahamas. Its scope transcends The Bahamas, however, and would serve well the education of citizens of the British Commonwealth and the United States of America.

With simple yet powerful language, the author has captured the essence of the life and times of the period factually, graphically and sensitively. A great read!"

DAME IVY DUMONT
Former Governor General of The Bahamas

"The elements could not be more conducive to a fascinating read: a world at war, a sleepy but strategically-located British colony, a great love story, a former king as governor of a tiny colony, political intrigue, the beginning of social upheaval. Sir Orville weaves all these elements together to produce a highly readable book, one that is bound to attract the attention of Bahamians and those interested in Bahamian history."

SIR ARTHUR FOULKES
Former Governor General of The Bahamas

"Gems of history from Mount Fitzwilliam by Sir Orville."

HARRY OAKES
Son of Sir Harry Oakes

"What Manner of Man Is This? is a story in a Bahamian context of the Duke of Windsor, who as king of England for ten months, created the scandal of the century when he gave up his throne for the 'woman I love.'

The only job that the Duke held after his abdication was as governor of The Bahamas, then a colony. For him it was banishment. For the British government it meant keeping him far from Europe and the German influence, as he was recorded as telling American editor and playwright, the late Fulton Oursler, that Hitler was not only the right and logical leader of the German people, but he was also a great man.

However, of even greater interest is this book's subplot—the life of the Bahamian people who lived back of the hill, but within a lifetime had crossed over the hill—and one of them, this book's author, had like the Duke before him—taken up residence in Mount Fitzwilliam, the official residence of the governor general of The Bahamas.

This is an historical work of a period in our country that should be in every Bahamian school, if only to impress upon young Bahamians the importance of taking the right turn in the road to their future so that they too can climb to the top of life's hill. Sir Orville's life and achievements should inspire young Bahamians, regardless of background, to also aim for the stars."

Eileen Carron
Editor/Publisher, The Tribune

WHAT MANNER OF MAN IS THIS?

WHAT MANNER OF MAN IS THIS?

The
DUKE OF WINDSOR'S
Years in The Bahamas

SIR ORVILLE TURNQUEST

GRANT'S TOWN PRESS | NASSAU, THE BAHAMAS

WHAT MANNER OF MAN IS THIS?

Copyright © 2016 by Orville A. Turnquest

GRANT'S TOWN PRESS
P O Box N 8181
Nassau NP
The Bahamas
www.grantstownpress.com

ISBN:
978-976-95976-0-0 Hardcover
978-976-95976-1-7 Paperback
978-976-95976-2-4 Ebook
Printed in the United States of America

First Edition

It is with much love and deep appreciation that I dedicate this book to my late dear wife, Edith.

She was involved in the early preparation and research when I began this literary project and she never ceased to encourage me along the way, remaining my steadfast motivation to complete this book.

I shall be forever grateful for the deep love and overwhelming support which Edith gave me throughout the many years that we shared together—from our days in high school, throughout all my ventures, and in rearing a wonderful family.

She is now happily enjoying her eternal rest. So, until we meet again, may she rest in peace.

And they feared exceedingly,
And said one to another,
What manner of man is this,
That even the wind and the sea obey him?

—MARK 4:41

CONTENTS

ACKNOWLEDGMENTS

I have often said that there are two other co-authors of this book.

First, I wish to especially thank Rowena Symonette for her decades of professionalism and devotion to me as my trusted colleague and cherished friend. She was by my side from the outset of this book and I could not have written one word without her most capable assistance and encouragement.

And deep appreciation to Diane Gedymin, my trusted editor and publisher for over a decade, who not only took my words and transformed them to make this book the best it could be and then made it a reality, but also became a dear friend and fellow citizen of The Bahamas.

My loyal and capable staff has always been there for me— Roslyn Bastian and Cpl. Brenton Charlton—who each never wavered in their dedication and commitment to both their official duties and to the completion of this book.

Jim Lawlor provided invaluable assistance in researching and documenting material in a most thorough way leaving no stone unturned in his search for information and sources.

Last but not least, my fondness and gratitude to my family and friends who have listened to promises to complete this book for ever so long but nevertheless maintained their faith in me and supported and encouraged me from the beginning, through the hard times, to the finish line.

My deepest appreciation to all who have taken this long journey with me. I could not have done it without each and every one of you.

FOREWORD

At the time the Duke of Windsor was appointed governor of The Bahamas in 1940, the majority native black population was completely subjugated under white minority rule. Although in those days the term apartheid was never uttered, every aspect of black Bahamian life was nevertheless controlled by the white oligarchs who ruled this segregated British colony. And make no mistake about it—from the moment the Duke set foot on the island nation, he chose to walk among that exclusively white, privileged class and sought to maintain the status quo for its black citizens.

Sir Orville Turnquest, a black Bahamian who eventually earned his way to occupying the very same office as the Duke, is in a special position to critically assess one of the most important world figures ever to hold the position of governor of The Bahamas in the history of the country. To his credit, Turnquest has not written a sanitized biography of the Duke of Windsor but rather an incisive examination of a small but enormously important slice of the life of this notorious man, a former king of England, who abdicated the throne to marry a divorced commoner—unheard of at the time—and then reluctantly accepted the position he was assigned in the remote Islands of The Bahamas.

More importantly, here is an unvarnished, fresh look at a crucial period of the Bahamian nation to which the Duke felt he was exiled during the tumultuous years preceding World War II. His appointment thus pushed this small country headlong onto the global stage at a time when pivotal and calamitous events were occurring there as well—The Bay Street Fire, The Burma Road Riot, the murder in Nassau of the wealthy Sir Harry Oakes, and programs undertaken with the United States that impacted both nations—the "Contract" and the "Project."

It is this largely ignored segment of the Duke's life that Sir Orville is particularly qualified to discuss, having grown up in Nassau during the time that the Duke was in office. And so did I. As classmates at Western Senior School, Orville—affectionately called Tiny at the time—and I were among the boys from "Over the Hill," the poor, black district that was segregated from the affluent white neighborhoods in all ways. He and I shared membership in a group of black boys from East Street and Grant's Town that did everything together—playing soccer, shooting marbles, flying kites, roller skating, and never missing a cowboy movie at the East Street Cinema, among other more mischievous youthful antics.

Somehow, through luck or character or fear of our fathers' ire, Orville and I managed to stay out of serious trouble in Nassau, but there were other children who were not as fortunate. Through their own foolish actions—or simply because youth with their color of skin were not welcomed on this or that street—many young boys were rounded up and sent to what were then called reform schools; repeat offenders were unceremoniously and often without representation thrown into jails among hardened adult criminals. These kids didn't stand a chance. The legal system of the day offered no consideration for black families' needs or well-being. Worse, the British colonial government represented by local rich white men showed neither respect for nor recognition of the basic human dignities of the country's black citizens.

Some families—a minuscule percentage of the population such

as small-business owners and religious leaders—were able to rise above the norm. Turnquest's father, for example, was a grocer and worked hard to ensure that his children were well educated. Fearing that I could fall in with the wrong crowd, my father felt that his only choice was to send me off to live with my older brother in Miami. In different ways, Orville and I were therefore spared this downward spiral, but we each had many friends and relatives who were not so lucky. In fact, I remember as a young boy jumping as high as I could to peer over the stone wall that surrounded the governor's mansion just to get a glimpse of an older brother who had been arrested for some minor infraction and whose sentence was forced labor as a gardener on the grounds of the Duke and Duchess's residence.

What makes this book stand out from the many books about the Duke and Duchess of Windsor is that when Sir Orville describes the hard life that the majority of black Bahamians experienced during those years—the racist culture, the lack of good education, the subsistence-level jobs if they were even lucky enough to have one, the dire living conditions, and the lack of full voting rights and adequate representation to address these very issues— he speaks knowledgeably and with the authenticity that only someone from that time and place can provide. When he takes the former king to task for doing little to nothing to address the racial disparity that existed at that time, he speaks passionately from the deep well of personal experience that only a young black boy from Over the Hill can feel.

And when he analyzes the few accomplishments and many failures of the Duke of Windsor's tenure in the office of Governor of The Bahamas, he speaks authoritatively from the experience of someone who has hands-on knowledge of the nuances of the office that both of these men held. And finally, when he assesses the Duke's legacy not only as royal governor but as a man, he speaks wisely as someone who was prohibited from residing on the other side of that hill but who, like me, probably leapt high to see over the stone wall of the governor's mansion—where no black man or woman, unless as a servant or worker, was allowed to officially enter during the Duke's tenure. A man who later became a husband and father and leader who was privileged to call home that very same mansion at the top of the hill that divided black from white.

Sir Orville Turnquest, orator, top litigator, and esteemed elder statesman as former governor general and head of state of The Bahamas, has shown the insight and courage to give his country and the world an extraordinary book about a man and a nation that converged at a critical time in global and Bahamian history.

—Sir Sidney Poitier

Strictly speaking, this book is not a biography of the Duke of Windsor during the years of his governorship of The Bahamas, though he is at its heart. In the same way that people define history itself, an outstanding personality often highlights the important events of a particular period—the plight of a nation, the reach of empathy, and the alignment of response. On the other hand, to focus purely on the history of The Bahamas during the years of World War II would exclude much of the texture contributed by the personality of Edward VIII, king and governor.

This book thus seeks to combine the history of a country and the biography of an exceptionally interesting and controversial man during a critical five-year period in Bahamian, British Commonwealth, and world history. It does so by knitting together pivotal local and global events, political developments, personal stories, and social challenges of the time.

Undoubtedly one of the most intriguing personalities in modern history, the Duke of Windsor remains a captivating subject for readers worldwide. As Prince of Wales and heir to the throne of what was undeniably the most powerful nation on earth at the beginning of the twentieth century, he was royally trained and nourished in the ways of kingship. During his youth and early manhood he travelled to all parts of an empire "on which the sun never set" as part of his preparation for becoming King Edward

VIII of Great Britain, Ireland, and the British Dominions beyond the Seas, King, Defender of the Faith, Emperor of India, and Sovereign of the Most Noble Order of the Garter.

Edward became king of England upon the death of his father, King George V, on January 20, 1936. He reigned for a mere ten months until that fateful day in December of that year when he signed the historic instrument of abdication. Renouncing his throne in order to marry the twice-divorced Mrs. Wallis Simpson, an American who had become his mistress and who now became his Duchess, he assumed his new title of Duke of Windsor. It was at once the scandal of the century and the love story of the age.

While many books have been written about this couple, the passion of their affair, and the circumstances that led the Duke to choose a life of exile in France rather than carry out his kingly duties without the help and support of the woman he loved being accepted as his queen, this book focuses on his administration while he served as governor and commander in chief of The Bahamas at a time when these now world-renowned "islands of paradise" were but a small colony of the British Empire. Certainly unimportant by any criteria and hardly known at the time, The Bahamas was physically and economically undeveloped with very limited educational or industrial opportunities for its citizens, and it openly exhibited the racial and discriminatory practices of the day to which black human beings were subjected in most parts of the world. For those who failed to recognize the country's many positive aspects, its one saving grace was its close proximity to the mainland of the United States.

The fact that such a famous man was posted to a small, remote island colony during the dramatic global events of the period led the United States and Britain to place a special focus on The Bahamas. This undoubtedly contributed greatly to the subsequent growth and development of the islands. During the war,

two programs had a lasting impact on both the United States and
The Bahamas: the Contract—the placement of thousands of black
Bahamians throughout the United States in special work pro-
grams; and the Project—the employment of Americans in The
Bahamas to work side by side with local labourers on airports crit-
ical to U.S. military strategy.

A few of the previous books about the Duke and Duchess have
included an examination of his term as governor of The Bahamas,
and even sought to praise the couple's positive involvement in
some aspects of life in the islands during the difficult years of
World War II. Without exception, however, all such publications
were written by authors using the documentary evidence available to them at the time, both official and otherwise, in order to
recount the achievements and the events in the lives of this glam-
orous and intriguing couple. These authors, moreover, have all
been non-Bahamians recording the Bahamian episode of the
Duke's story from secondary sources.

This book is unique in that I am particularly qualified to address
the historical subject. As a black Bahamian, I was an eleven-year-old
student in August 1940 when the Duke of Windsor was sworn in as
the fifty-fifth governor of the Colony of The Bahamas. In January
1995, I too was sworn in as the seventieth in the chain of succession, becoming the fifth Bahamian governor general of an independent Bahamas. The Duke and I thus both shared the distinction
of serving in a direct line of succession since 1670 as representative
heads of state of this small archipelagic country.

In my official capacity, first as a Bahamian cabinet minister
and later as governor general, I had frequent occasions to interact
with members of the Royal Family, both at Buckingham Palace
and nearby Windsor Castle. In addition, I occasionally met with
Queen Elizabeth and various other members of the Royal Family
during both their royal and private visits to The Bahamas.

As governor general of The Bahamas for almost seven years, my official role was to function as the representative head of state on behalf of Her Majesty who, as Queen of The Bahamas, is technically also Head of State of The Bahamas. She is likewise also Queen of Canada, Australia, Jamaica, and those other independent countries of the British Commonwealth of Nations that were former colonies, but upon their attaining independence, chose to retain a monarchial, rather than a republican, form of government.

This book examines in detail the lives, the record, and the actions of the Duke and Duchess in their roles as governor and governor's wife of The Bahamas during one of the most tumultuous eras in both this island nation and in world history.

Viewed with the advantage of my first-hand perspective, I am able to credit the Duke with doing much to improve and develop the economic base of the country. To the contrary, however, I regret that there were areas of the Duke's failure as a royal governor where he did not even attempt to do those things he ought to have done.

This book shows him as a racially biased individual, unwilling to disturb the status quo and, in light of his undisputed influence and world stature, one who fell far short of implementing positive social changes which cried out to be made. During the five-year term of his administration he was content to work and socialize with the white oligarchic minority—which comprised only fifteen percent of the Bahamian population—and to accept their strictly enforced discriminatory practices. Unfortunately the Duke was equally content to leave the black communities as unequal in every way as when he first met them.

Since I later occupied the same office, represented the same people, and even slept under the same roof in the governor's mansion, I often felt a natural awareness of what must have been many of the Duke's challenges, and was thus able to examine each official action—and even his personal ones—from a unique point of view.

In reviewing the Duke's tenure as governor of The Bahamas, which was the only job he ever held after giving up the throne of England, I believe that I have provided a fair commentary on his performance and have shown what manner of man England's most famous royal duke really was.

—Sir Orville Turnquest

PART 1

HIS APPOINTMENT

WHAT MANNER OF
MAN IS THIS?

The Duke was born on June 23, 1894, the firstborn son of King George V and Queen Mary. His great-grandmother, Queen Victoria, was then the reigning monarch of the United Kingdom and the British Dominions and Colonies, and Empress of India. The Archbishop of Canterbury, the Reverend Edward White Benson, baptized the royal infant in the Green Drawing Room of White Lodge on July 16, 1894. He was given the names Edward Albert Christian George Andrew Patrick David, and was known as His Highness Prince Edward of York. The first name was chosen in tribute to his late uncle, who was known to his family as Eddie, and the third name was for his great-grandfather King Christian IX of Denmark. The name Albert was included at the request of Queen Victoria in honour of her late husband. The last four names represented the patron saints of England, Scotland, Ireland, and Wales. Notwithstanding the rich legacy he thus carried by his seven names, he was nevertheless always known to his family and close friends simply as David.

Upon Queen Victoria's death on January 22, 1901, at the age of eighty-one, she was succeeded by her eldest son, who became King Edward VII, the Duke's grandfather, who was in turn succeeded in 1910 by Prince Edward's own father, King George V. At that time, Edward, a boy of sixteen, then became His Royal Highness the Prince of Wales, successor to the throne of England, having earlier been known as HRH Prince Edward of Wales, and subsequently HRH the Duke of Cornwall.

Although the Duke's father was known to be even more affectionate towards his children than their mother, and his grandparents, Queen Alexandra and King Edward VII, were likewise extremely affectionate, King George V was thought to be excessively strict with regard to their upbringing and royal training, especially in respect of their dress, speech, and social form.

Despite the family affection that was exhibited toward the young prince, like other upper-class children of the period, Edward was brought up by nannies rather than directly by his parents. On one occasion, when Edward was not cooperating as he was being prepared to be presented to his parents, one of his nannies disciplined him with a pinch. His father's strictness apparently did not apply to physical punishment meted out by the young prince's caretakers; his subsequent crying led to the woman's prompt discharge and Edward remained particularly resistant to nanny scoldings.

Edward received his early education by being tutored at home by a nurse named Helen Bricker, and later by Frederick Finch and Henry Hansell, who also taught his brothers and sister. Edward received some form of private tutorship until he was almost thirteen years old. In 1907 he entered Osborne Naval College, which served as training for his later service in the British Armed Forces.

By then heir to the British throne and anxious to demonstrate his loyalty and capability, in June 1914 Edward joined the Grenadier Guards, the most senior regiment in the British Army. When

World War I broke out the very next month, he applied for active duty and was keen to be involved in actual combat. However, the secretary of state for war, Lord Kitchener, realizing that should the future king of England be captured by the enemy the result would entail immense diplomatic difficulties, refused to allow him to be stationed on the front lines. Nevertheless, the Duke did witness intense active warfare. In the Battle of the Somme he rubbed shoulders with foot soldiers in the trenches while fighting the Germans. Appalled at the dire conditions under which the armed forces were compelled to live, he visited the front-line soldiers as often as he could. As a result of this involvement he attained the rank of lieutenant, and was awarded the Military Cross in 1916. He also took training as a pilot with the Royal Air Force, and in 1918 made his first military flight. This active service and dedication to his fellow soldiers made him very popular amongst war veterans.

The tradition of military training and service among the Royal Family has continued to the present day. Prince William, Duke of Cambridge and his brother Prince Harry (Prince Henry of Wales), sons of the Duke of Windsor's great-nephew, Prince Charles, the present heir to the throne, have both served in the British Army and attained the rank of captain. Indeed, Prince Harry has experienced wartime service in Afghanistan and has been awarded the Operational Service Medal, and both princes have received the Queen's Golden Jubilee Medal.

During the 1920s, the Duke travelled extensively on behalf of his father to various parts of the British Empire, including Canada, where he acquired a ranch to which he was to return on several occasions in later years. His royal tours included a myriad of countries such as New Zealand, Australia, Fiji, Samoa, Hawaii, Mexico, Panama, Trinidad, British Guyana, the Windward and the Leeward Islands, and Bermuda, all of which he visited in 1920 alone.

This was followed by additional trips in 1921 to Gibraltar, Malta, Egypt, Aden, India, Burma, Ceylon, Malaya, Hong Kong, Japan, the Philippines, and British North Borneo. In 1923 and 1924 he returned to Canada and the United States. In 1925 he visited most of the countries in Africa, as well as Saint Helena and other countries in South America. During the period of 1927–1930 he confined his travels to countries in Africa; in 1931 he returned to countries in South America; and from 1932–1936 he visited most of the countries of Europe.[1]

This continuous and intensive spate of royal visits made him the most photographed public figure of his time. One of the world's most popular and handsome bachelors, the Duke was also reputed to have had relationships with a steady stream of older, attractive, and sometimes married women. Beyond this wide international recognition, he soon assumed even greater stature.

At five minutes before midnight on January 20, 1936, King George V died. His oldest son, Edward, as Prince of Wales and heir to the throne, immediately thereupon became King of England and the British Empire. It is reported that upon realizing that his father had passed and that he had become king, his grief was overwhelming, displayed in somewhat frantic and hysterical outbursts of crying.[2]

Edward ascended to the English throne as King Edward VIII, the monarch of what was then the most powerful nation in the world, and sovereign head of the British Empire that then comprised a myriad of land masses, islands, and cays that spanned the earth. Indeed it was said that "the sun never sets on the British Empire," owing to the fact that some part of it was always experiencing daylight.

1 P. Ziegler, *King Edward VIII*, New York, Alfred A Kopf, Inc., 1990, p. 209.
2 Ibid., p. 210.

As was customary for centuries, preparation for the royal coronation began soon after Edward became king. In actual fact, under British law he assumed all the accompanying rights and privileges of kingship immediately upon the death of his father. A coronation would therefore be the formal, public celebration marking this historic event. Since Edward was undoubtedly more well travelled and widely known across the globe than any monarch before him, the preparation and accommodation for this world-class event was intended to include persons representing nations from every part of the globe.

In addition to his global presence, King Edward VIII had been well prepared and trained for his accession to this unique and powerful post in other ways. He was also endowed with personal qualities which particularly suited him for his royal role—he was considered handsome with considerable charm and good speaking abilities. Through his travels he had acquired a broad range of first-hand knowledge of the ways, customs, and needs of the people residing in most of the widespread Empire he now ruled.

Prime Minister Stanley Baldwin, upon formally announcing the death and the accession to the House of Commons, pointed out that aspect of the king's experience when he declared that

"King Edward VIII brings to the altar of public service a personality richly endowed with the experience of public affairs, with the fruits of travel and universal goodwill. He has the secret of youth in the prime of age. He has a wider and more intimate knowledge of all classes of his subjects . . . than any of his predecessors."[3]

Upon assuming this high regal office, because he was already so well known and beloved both at home and abroad, the king

3 Ziegler, p. 210.

was not required to appear in public frequently. He did, however, carry out a busy daily calendar of appointments and events despite the existing official restrictions resulting from the court mourning that officially followed the death of his father. He was continually occupied with meetings with his cabinet ministers, mayors of various British cities, military officers, colonial governors, and other country officials.

Although the royal calendar was in this way always full, King Edward was also obliged to meet "privileged bodies," key leaders of the community who under an ancient right were granted the opportunity to present their "loyal addresses" to a new king upon his ascent to the throne. These introductions had for centuries been made during a private reception with the king during which each of the leaders, following a fixed ritual, confirmed his loyalty to the throne. When inquiring how many persons he was required to meet, he was advised that he should expect about twenty delegations, which included heads of the many national universities, royal societies, banks, corporations, religious communities, and the Royal Academy of Arts.[4]

To more efficiently meet this obligation Edward reduced the time required to see each of these groups separately by arranging to receive them collectively. This seemingly small change was actually quite a departure from royal tradition and was just one example of the new king's attempt to modernize some of the ancient traditions and privileges which had existed for centuries. Not every divergence from royal custom was seen in that light. In fact, his nonconformist propensity became the hallmark of his later history in contrast to his earlier public life.

In years past, as he trekked across the world stage as one of its most famous and admired men, he had portrayed the essence of

---

4 Ziegler, p. 219.

royal stature and power. His charm and influence were legendary. Men and women adored him, and wherever he went, his every word commanded unwavering attention and a positive response, and his every wish was fulfilled. Soon, however, having reached its apex, his star began to fall.

King Edward's affair and intensifying love for Wallis Warfield Simpson, a twice-married American socialite who had divorced her first husband and was in the process of divorcing her second, was not widely known at the time and far from becoming the worldwide scandal into which it developed a mere ten months later. From the moment that he acceded to the throne, Edward VIII seemed determined to keep his private life separate and distinct from his public persona, and was known to declare that his private life was his own.[5]

This, of course, was impossible for the king of England, especially since, from the outset of his reign, he focused great attention and extravagant generosity on Mrs. Simpson, which led to growing suspicion among those officials and courtiers with whom he was in daily contact, particularly among the aristocracy and nobility nearest to him.

The most troublesome in a series of King Edward's aberrations from royal protocol occurred when he proposed marriage to Mrs. Simpson. Although he could have legally married her and remained monarch, the prime ministers of the various dominions in the Empire opposed the marriage on the grounds that the people of their countries would never accept the divorced Mrs. Simpson as queen. Moreover, as nominal head of the Church of England, Edward would also be breaking Church codes by marrying a woman whose two ex-husbands were still living.

A political crisis emerged as well since he had been warned that should he proceed with the marriage while still reigning as

5 Ziegler, p. 216.

monarch, Prime Minister Stanley Baldwin and his cabinet would resign, resulting in a general election and the resultant irreparable damage to the constitutional monarchy's status as always politically neutral.

It is interesting to contrast the prevailing attitudes and traditions of society in the 1930s with those commonplace today, some eighty years later. For the king of England to even propose taking a twice-divorced woman as his wife was then quite unacceptable if not unthinkable. Although embroiled in a scandal that similarly captured the world's attention, Charles, likewise Prince of Wales, remains the present heir to the same throne of England. Although he divorced his late first wife, the globally beloved Princess Diana, and subsequently married his present wife, Camilla, who herself is a divorcée, Prince Charles has not been forced to choose between love and crown.

King Edward was allowed no such freedom. Rather than give up his love, his fiancée Mrs. Wallis Simpson, he chose to abdicate the throne.

THE ABDICATION

On December 10, 1936, Edward VIII, King of England and the British Empire, stunned his own nation and the world with his decision to abdicate the throne for the woman he loved. The astounding communication was formally announced to the British Parliament by Prime Minister Stanley Baldwin. Although preparations had been in progress over the preceding eleven months since he was named king, Edward's reign ended before his coronation actually occurred.

The preceding days of that week had been filled with drama, tension, and sometimes faint hope that he would change his mind; but in the end nothing would shake the king's determination as a series of hurried meetings took place among members of the Royal Family, ministers of the overseas dominions of the British Empire, and between Prime Minister Baldwin and the king.

The final day preceding the abdication announcement was permeated with a sense of gloom; the British cabinet sat for two and one-half hours without arriving at any positive or preventative step, as more and more it became evident that the monarch's desire to relinquish the throne was irreversible. At the cabinet meeting on the Wednesday, Prime Minister Baldwin reported the king's "firm and definite intention to renounce the throne,"[6] and in a letter written after this meeting the prime minister made his last appeal to his sovereign. In reply to this letter the king wrote: "His Majesty has given the matter his further consideration, but regrets that he is unable to alter his decision."[7]

It was this reply that the prime minister reported to a tense and hushed House of Commons on Thursday afternoon, while thousands of people, in a sombre and quiet atmosphere, stood outside the Houses of Parliament in London.

The last words of King Edward VIII, as king speaking to his subjects, were delivered in his farewell broadcast from Windsor Castle at ten o'clock on Friday morning, December 11, 1936. In a voice that was thick and tired, he delivered his historic abdication speech, including the now-famous passage which will always be quoted as a declaration of the force and vibrancy of true love:

". . . but you must believe me when I tell you that I have found it impossible to carry the heavy burden of responsibility and discharge my duties as king as I would wish to do without the help and support of the woman I love."

Later came his final, closing declaration: "I now quit altogether public affairs, and I lay down my burden."[8]

After delivering his final speech as monarch, no longer King Edward VIII, he left Windsor Castle as Prince Edward and

6 Ziegler, p. 280.

7 Ibid.

8 R. G. Martin, *The Woman He Loved,* New York, Simon and Schuster, 1974, pp. 293–294.

travelled to Portsmouth where he embarked on a British destroyer, HMS *Fury*, which was waiting to carry him across the English Channel. Accompanied by his equerry and a detective, he disembarked at Boulogne and, with dozens of newspaper reporters and photographers in tow, travelled by train to Vienna, Austria, to begin a new life in his self-imposed exile.

Next in line to the throne was Albert, Duke of York, the eldest of Edward's younger brothers. Upon acceding to the throne, following the regal custom of taking the name of one of his familial predecessors, Albert chose his father's name to become King George VI. He began his reign at 1:52 p.m. on December 11, 1936. With other members of the family he had tried forcefully to dissuade Edward from pursuing his intended purpose to abdicate, but to no avail.[9]

On the Friday afternoon following the abdication broadcast, their mother, Queen Mary, also presented a public message to her son's subjects, acknowledging the immeasurable amount of sympathy which had been given to her. The Queen Mother, as was now her official title, stated that "I need not speak to you of the distress which fills a mother's heart when I think that my dear son has deemed it to be his duty to lay down his charge, and that the reign which had begun with so much hope and promise has so suddenly ended." Without dwelling further on her personal grief or the current national disaster, Queen Mary then continued: "I commend to you his brother, summoned so unexpectedly and in circumstances so painful, to take his place . . ."[10]

As news of the abdication spread over the country and the world at large, the popularity and the strong affection in which King Edward was held worldwide engendered both sympathy

9 Ziegler, p. 285.

10 Martin, p. 301.

(and relief) by most people at this critical period in British history. However, a public condemnation was broadcast the following Sunday, December 13, 1936, when the Archbishop of Canterbury, the Right Reverend Dr. Cosmo Gordon Lang, preached a sermon in the Concert Hall of Broadcasting House in London in which he strongly rebuked the former king for abdicating a high and sacred trust and craving private happiness in a manner inconsistent with the Christian principles of marriage.[11]

Earlier Dr. Lang had likewise stated on film that he had the greatest doubts about the sanctity of the king's intended marriage to Mrs. Simpson and indicated that it was potentially a resignation issue.[12] Both the king and Prime Minister Baldwin knew of the archbishop's views, and it was widely assumed at the time that Dr. Lang had played a leading role in forcing the king out. Lang's radio transmission after the abdication, which was widely seen as "kicking Edward VIII when he is down,"[13] most likely helped to cement the public belief that Lang was the key figure in the abdication crisis.

Included among the myriad of newspaper commentaries that chronicled what has been described as "the greatest love story of the century" was another negative commentary, which appeared in the *Nassau Daily Tribune*, published in The Bahamas the day after the abdication was announced to the public. This editorial was republished in a newspaper in Atlanta, Georgia, where it received wide publicity because of the impact and impression which it made, especially coming from what was described as a little newspaper published in a tiny corner of the British Empire.

The *Tribune* had commented:

---

11 Martin, p. 263.

12 Ibid.

13 Ibid., p. 305.

"Edward, the king whom the whole world loved, respected and admired; the king whom the Empire needed most at this time and from whom the Empire expected so much, yesterday meekly faced the microphone—this mature man of 42—and told the whole world that he had laid down 'the heavy burden of responsibility' for the woman he loved, a pitiable appeal for sympathy from a man to whom the Empire had looked to infuse in its veins a new life, a new ambition, greater strength and courage to face its gathering enemies and carry the Empire to a still higher plane of glory and accomplishment. This is a bitter pill for British people to swallow.

"As king, history must deal with him severely. It must send his name down to posterity as the king who had the greatest opportunity for service as any man who has ever lived, but who sought the easy way in the arms of a woman, with money he inherited from the Nation . . . a woman with a history that made all thought of her taking the place of Queen Mary on the throne repugnant to British peoples throughout the world.

"As a man, Edward has placed himself in the greatest story of all time, deserving the pen of a Shakespeare. A great deal of blame is being laid on the woman. We are all hunters of one sort or another. Right in Nassau we see men and women sacrificing their souls for some vain empty honour, some inconsequential dignity. Miss Simpson [*sic*] has hunted and won not only another man, but a place in history as the woman who might have sat on the throne of England . . . and who might have wrecked the greatest Empire of all time. Suffice it to say that had she been worth the sacrifice she would not have allowed her lover to make it.

"Today, more than ever, we owe it to George VI to rally around his banner and echo with a loud voice his cry, 'Excelsior!' To Edward we say . . . may God help you to find the happiness you seek in the fickle smile of a woman, and spare you an awakening to a full realization of the true significance of your irrevocable decision."[14]

These pointed remarks were written by the late Sir Etienne Dupuch, who, at the time of the abdication, had been the publisher and editor of the *Nassau Daily Tribune* (later changed to just *The Tribune*) since 1919. In a professional career spanning seventy-two years, his editorial career commenced when he returned from overseas service as a soldier in the British Army during World War I, and he retired in 1972, continuing as the paper's contributing editor until his death in 1991. On that historic date in 1936 Sir Etienne was, in his journalistic capacity, and like all other worldwide observers of the current political developments in Britain at that time, commenting on what was undoubtedly the most newsworthy world event of the period.

For six months following the abdication, Prince Edward remained in exile in Austria and France, making preparations for his marriage to Mrs. Simpson. The wedding took place in Candé, in France, on Thursday, June 3, 1937, first with a civil ceremony to conform with the requirements of French law, followed immediately thereafter by a private religious ceremony conducted in the music room of their borrowed residence Chateau de Candé, near Tours, by the Reverend Robert Anderson Jardine. The Reverend Jardine, a Church of England vicar of St. Paul's Church, Darlington, an industrial parish near Durham in North West England, had offered to perform the ceremony after he learned that the Church of England refused to sanction the union. The new King, George VI, similarly disapproved of the impending marriage, and thus forbade members of the Royal Family to

14 E. Dupuch, "Editorial: The Greatest Love Story of the Century," *Nassau Daily Tribune*, 12 December 1936.

attend the wedding. Edward had particularly wanted his brothers the Dukes of Gloucester and Kent, and his second cousin, Lord Louis Mountbatten (after 1947 Earl Mountbatten of Burma) to be there. The royal prohibition for visitations continued for many years, infuriating the Duke and Duchess of Windsor.

Whether sympathizer or critic, friend or foe, royal or commoner, no one in the world, including those in remote and little-known outposts of the Empire such as The Bahamas, could possibly have imagined that a mere three and one-half years following the abdication, these islands would be catapulted into the focus of world attention when British prime minister Winston Churchill appointed the former king of England to govern this tiny colony. Having been accorded the formal title of Duke of Windsor, he was also to become the governor and commander in chief of the Bahama Islands, a post which he arrived to assume on August 8, 1940, accompanied by his wife, the former Wallis Warfield Simpson, now Duchess of Windsor.

THE DUCHESS

Prior to World War II and the period of the abdication, the crowned heads of Europe and Asia and their families were still considered a special breed whose royal blood and accompanying rights and privileges caused them to be regarded and respected as a cut above ordinary citizens. As a member of this rarified group, and as the heir apparent to the throne of the British Empire, Edward was considered as perhaps the most eligible bachelor on the face of the earth. It was certainly expected that he would choose the future queen of England from a select array of equally majestic and noble-blooded women who could proudly be regaled and accepted as queen by all levels of society, government, and church.

Instead, against all such expectations and generations of royal practice, the woman of the Duke's affections was Wallis Warfield Simpson, a nonaristocratic, twice-divorced woman, both of whose ex-husbands were still living. Although Mrs. Simpson was found by most to be totally unacceptable to become the wife of the king of England, Edward was smitten and chose to ignore all of these grave concerns.

Although she did indeed marry the former king of England on June 3, 1937, the Duchess of Windsor was never formally accorded the status of a royal personage. In fact, mere days prior to their wedding, the Duke's brother and successor, King George VI, approved a decision by the British government which led to the following announcement, printed in the *London Gazette* on May 29, 1937:

"The King has been pleased by letters patent under the great seal of the realm, bearing the date of 27th May, 1937, to declare that the Duke of Windsor shall, notwithstanding an instrument of abdication, executed on the 10th day of December, 1936, and His Majesty's Declaration of the Abdication Act of 1936, whereby effect was given to the said instrument, be entitled to hold and enjoy for himself only the title, style or attribute of Royal Highness so, however, that his wife and descendants, if any, shall not hold said title, style or attribute."[15]

Many years later Sir Dudley Forwood, who at the time was the Duke's equerry—an officer of the British royal household charged with his care—reported that when the Duke became aware of this decision, "He put down his beautiful head with its golden hair in my lap and sobbed helplessly. His heart was broken and in a sense it never healed."[16]

Bessie Wallis Warfield was born on June 19, 1896, the only child of Alice Montague Warfield and Teackle Wallis Warfield, the youngest son of Henry Mactier Warfield, a wealthy flower

15 Announcement, *London Gazette,* 29 May, 1937.

16 C. Higham, *The Duchess of Windsor, The Secret Life,* New York, McGraw Hill Book Company, 1988, p. 217.

merchant and popular citizen of Baltimore, Maryland. Although born into a socially prominent and affluent American family, when Wallis was only five months old her father died at age twenty-five, leaving his young wife penniless.

Bessie and her mother were financially provided for by members of her father's family, primarily his wealthy bachelor brother, Solomon Davies Warfield, who was postmaster of Baltimore and later president of two prominent companies. She and her mother initially lived with him in a four-story mansion, which his mother also shared, but in 1901, when Alice's older sister, Bessie Merryman, was widowed, Bessie and her mother moved in to live with her for a year or so, until they moved and settled in a home of their own. At her birth, she was in fact named in honour of this aunt and continued to be called Bessie Wallis throughout her youth until she eventually dropped her first name. Because the name was popularly associated with cows, Wallis decided it did not suit her. In 1908 her mother married her second husband, John Freeman Rasin.

All in all, Wallis experienced a fairly happy childhood with the usual privileges, quality education, and training given to teenagers of well-off families of the period. Reports indicate that she was an extremely bright student who always excelled over her classmates, and she grew up to be an individual who was independent, exceptional, and outstanding.[17]

While visiting a female cousin in Pensacola, Florida, in April 1916, Wallis met Earl Winfield Spencer, Jr., a U.S. Navy pilot whom she married seven months later on November 8, 1916, in Baltimore when she was twenty years of age.[18] The marriage, however, was an extremely unhappy one. Spencer's increasingly

17 Higham, *The Duchess of Windsor,* p. 12.

18 Ibid., pp. 30–39.

high alcohol intake, stemming from his strong dissatisfaction with his military involvement, led to many instances of abusive treatment. As a result, they separated in 1921 and again in 1922.[19]

During the second separation, Wallis had an affair with an Argentine diplomat, Felipe de Espil, who the Duchess later described as being only a little older than herself and "a man of great promise, who was intelligent, ambitious, subtle, gracious and in many respects the most fascinating man" she had ever met.[20]

Nevertheless, during the time her husband was stationed in the Far East, from 1922 until 1925, Wallis did travel to China to rejoin him in an effort to revive their marriage. On the contrary, reports have surfaced that while on her journey across the Pacific Ocean on the USS *Chaumont* on her way to China, she provided sexual favours to members of the ship's crew.[21] And it has also been said that during that visit she met and had an affair with Count Galeazzo Ciano, a foreign minister of Italy, by whom she became pregnant, leading to a botched abortion that left her unable to conceive. These tawdry stories were buttressed by rumors that during her year-long stay in China from 1924 to 1925, she frequented Chinese brothels where she acquired the art of sexually pleasing a man in other than traditional ways.[22]

These scandalous comments are not supported by the majority of historians. In December 1927 Wallis and her first husband, Earl Spencer, were indeed finally divorced.

By this time she had already become involved with Ernest Aldrich Simpson, a shipping executive, who was an American-born

19 Higham, pp. 29–30.

20 Martin, p. 70.

21 Ziegler, p. 195.

22 Ibid.

citizen living in London, where he operated the British office of his father's shipping business. Wallis married Ernest Simpson in July 1928, after which they made their home in the affluent district of Mayfair, London. The Simpsons soon became part of a social group comprising royalty and members of London's high society, and were regularly included in the circle of friends of Prince Edward. In fact, she met her future royal spouse during the fall of 1930 at one such social gathering after his return from a trip to South America. He and his brother Albert, later to become King George VI, as well as Mrs. Simpson and her husband, were all guests in the same house for a weekend fox hunt in Leicestershire, England.[23]

During the next few years they continued to meet occasionally as guests of mutual friends in London, and through these encounters Edward grew increasingly attracted and fond of her, gradually realizing that he must share his life with her. Wallis, on the other hand, could not understand why the prince, who could have had his pick among any of the world's most attractive women, was drawn to her as she herself admitted that she was neither beautiful nor young. She attributed his attraction to her independent spirit, and her inquisitiveness about him and things pertaining to him. She also credited herself with the ability to ease his loneliness. Wallis was enticed by the prince's charm, his personality and the warmth of his manner, and most certainly by the fact that he provided an introduction to a new and exciting stage in her life that she had never experienced or could have anticipated. She also admired the fact that he commanded attention and admiration, respect and obedience, seemingly without any effort. She was delighted to revel in his attentions.

Edward did not, however, enter into this love affair blindly; from the outset he fully knew that having his hope to marry

23 Higham, pp. 62–64.

her fulfilled would have many complications and serious consequences. The infamous Wallis Warfield Simpson has been the
subject of numerous published works in which she was often
accused of many unpleasant involvements. Another allegation
in *The Guardian* with the scandalous headline, "Car Dealer Was
Wallis Simpson's Secret Lover," stated that "Wallis Simpson kept
a secret lover—a Ford car salesman—while conducting a passionate affair with the future King Edward VIII, according to
special branch files [released in 2003] that reveal she was under
close surveillance."[24] She has even been vilified as a Russian spy, a
German spy, an Italian spy, and an American spy.

These and many more harsh accusations about her may or may
not be true, but what is fact is that Edward, the king of England,
followed his heart's desire. He abdicated his throne in order to
marry and Wallis became the Duchess of Windsor, his wife and
soul mate for the rest of his life.

24 O. Bowcott & S. Bates, "Car Dealer Was Wallis Simpson's Secret Lover."
The Guardian (UK) 30 January, 2003, pp. 1–2.

THE BAHAMAS

For more than a century before the abdication, advertisements designed to attract winter residents and vacationers to The Bahamas had dubbed the archipelago the Perpetual Isles of June. Visitors, mostly from the United States but also including large numbers of Canadians and Britons, regularly frequented the Bahamian shores during the winter months to enjoy the country's balmy weather, its spectacular beaches, and its lively musical entertainment, which was a special feature provided as a tourist attraction.

Visitors and residents alike have regularly heard local troubadours singing popular island melodies such as "Mama, Bahama Mama," hailing the perfection of the Bahamian climate in its tropical setting of fragrance and beauty. An example of the faster tempo of the regional musical style widely known as the West Indian calypso, the Bahamian tunes were called goombay songs, associated with the type of music played on similarly named goatskin drums that were beaten with the hands. These popular songs were featured in all of the many nightclubs in Nassau in the 1930s and 1940s, which the visitors and locals frequented, such as Dirty Dick's, Blackbeard's, Spider Web Club, Adastra Gardens, Silver Slipper, Coconut Palm, Cat & Fiddle, Conch Shell, and the Zanzibar. Despite the war, the Windsor years in The Bahamas were generally happy and carefree, albeit somewhat unsophisticated.

Those who looked for local nightlife excitement were entertained by the popular Bahamian musical stars of that era such as Blind Blake, George Symonette, Freddie Munnings, Charlie Adamson, Rudy Williams, and Lou Adams. In fact, Adams, now in his late eighties, together with fellow octogenarian Eric Cash, a revered and talented member of his orchestra, are the two survivors of a group of legendary musicians of a golden era in The Bahamas. With his trumpet and orchestra, to this day Adams still performs nightly at the exclusive Lyford Cay Club in the western end of New Providence Island. His band member Cash deftly handles the bass fiddle for the most part, but he also occasionally substitutes on the keyboard, at which he is also very adept, being the accomplished organist for decades at Our Lady of the Holy Souls Catholic Church.

From the late 1930s through the '40s, the Bahama Islands were fast becoming a tourist-based economy. Other local songs of the time likewise showed the increasingly more important place that tourism held in the country's economy, such as the tune entitled "Little Nassau," by famous calypso musician Blake Alphonso Higgs, better known as Blind Blake (1915–1986).

For centuries before the advent of tourism the islands were famed for their historical significance as the first landfall of Christopher Columbus in the Western world. On October 12, 1492, the Admiral of the Ocean Sea and Viceroy of the Western Indies, as he was later dubbed by King Ferdinand and Queen Isabella of Spain, first sighted the island of San Salvador, one of the smallest in the picturesque group of a 750-mile-long chain of approximately 700 islands and 2,500 small, limestone-formed islets or cays (pronounced *keys*).

This Atlantic Ocean archipelago stretches in a southeasterly arch from Abaco, the northernmost part of the island group, lying just forty-five miles off the city of Palm Beach on the east coast of south Florida. The group continues through 100,000 square miles of some of the most pristine waters in the world, down to Inagua, its most south-eastern island, which lies just north of the Turks and Caicos, a small group of islands geographically part of the Bahamian archipelago. After being administered as a British colony and a formal part of the Bahama Islands since 1799, a petition was sent to the British government in 1848 by the Turks and Caicos residents, after which these islands became a separate colony under the guidance of the governor of Jamaica in 1872. The islands remained annexed to Jamaica until 1962 when they were again linked administratively to The Bahamas by having their internal government headed by the governor of The Bahamas. When The Bahamas achieved its independence in 1973, however, the Turks and Caicos Islands remained a separate crown colony of Great Britain with their own governor.

The lower border of the Bahamian group of islands lies fifty miles to the north of the Caribbean islands of Cuba and Hispaniola, this latter island itself being shared by two separate countries, Haiti and the Dominican Republic.

Despite the great number of islands in the Bahamian chain, only some thirty of the larger islands are inhabited, with small communities and villages; New Providence, with its capital city of Nassau, and Grand Bahama, with the tourist and industrial town of Freeport, are the most highly populated among them.

Over the years poets, writers, and artists have continued to extol the physical and climatic excellence of The Bahamas. Today, five centuries after Columbus made his memorable voyage, his picturesque description of these islands, which he embodied in a letter to his sponsors the king and queen of Spain, still does justice to their beauty.

"The Country," Columbus wrote, "excels all others as far as the day surpasses the night and splendour; the natives love their neighbours as themselves; and so sweet and affectionate are they, that I swear to your Highnesses there is not a better place in all the world."[25]

Except for the letters of Columbus, the writings of Bartolemé de Las Casas, a Dominican priest who knew Columbus and was the editor of the admiral's journal and the logs of a few other early seagoing Spanish voyagers, surprisingly little is known of the earliest known inhabitants of these islands in Columbian and pre-Columbian times. It is believed that the Lucayans were of Arawak origin, and migrated northward from the region near the mouth of the Venezuelan Orinoco River by way of the "stepping stones" provided by the series of small islands now known as the Lesser Antilles, finally reaching Haiti and The Bahamas.

There is, however, nothing to disprove the popular theory that there was also a racial mixture of settlers coming from what is now the southeastern part of the United States, possibly by way of Cuba, or directly across the Straits of Florida to the western islands of The Bahamas. Indeed, the geographical position of the islands makes it extremely probable that the culture of the islands was distinctly affected by that of southeastern North America, as well as by the Mayan influence of the Yucatan.

It is known that the Lucayans were bold seafarers, and thus it is very unlikely that the forty-five-mile passage of the Florida

25 M. Craton & G. Saunders, *Islanders in the Stream,* vol. 2, Gainesville, University of Georgia Press, 1998, p. 48.

Straits presented any great barrier between them and the mainland. As it would only have been a day's journey for the speedy canoes known to have been developed in the islands, it is inconceivable that they would not have known of such a great land mass so near to the west (and vice versa). The museum and library located just south of Deadman's Cay in the settlement of Buckley's on Long Island is home to a significant quantity of relics and artifacts which have been identified as belonging to the Lucayan era. This archaeological evidence establishes that the pre-Columbian settlers were of Arawak origin.

At any rate, it was indeed the Lucayans who welcomed Columbus as he made his historic landfall, a date formerly called Columbus Day. It was later changed to Discovery Day but in 2013 it was officially designated as National Heroes Day, a public holiday honoring a wide range of outstanding Bahamian citizens. Columbus had set out from Spain, sailing westward across the Atlantic in search of gold and spices and other riches, convinced that he would reach the eastern shores of Cathay and Cipango. After a challenging voyage of seventy-one days in his flagship caravel the *Santa Maria*, accompanied by the *Niña* and the *Pinta*, Columbus and his crew were the first visitors from Europe to travel to The Bahamas, which he claimed for the Kingdom of Spain.

The Spaniards quickly followed this discovery with further incursions into the American mainland and, a few years later, conquered Mexico and a considerable portion of South America. The main motive of the subsequent voyages of geographical exploration and adventure was to discover and seize gold, silver, and precious stones to be sent back to Spain in their stately galleons or treasure ships.

At the end of the fifteenth century England was not yet a maritime power. However, fifty years later the now famous names of merchant adventurers such as Cabot, Frobisher, Hawkins, and Drake had come on the scene and challenged the Spanish treasure fleets with unrivaled valour and great success, culminating in the defeat of the Spanish Armada in the English Channel and the North Sea in 1588.

For the next century and a half, beginning with the attempt by Sir Walter Raleigh in 1585, the English colonies were settled in the New World by men and women who left England to escape religious intolerance and disputes, in search of adventure, or in hope of financial gain. King Charles I of England granted The Bahamas—together with a large territory, South Virginia, on the American mainland—to Sir Robert Heath, then the attorney general of England. Four years later Cardinal Richelieu granted five of the islands to prominent Frenchmen.[26] These grants did not result in permanent settlement.

Further colonization of the islands of The Bahamas was attempted by members of William Sayle's Eleutheran Adventurers, who were seeking escape from religious persecution. Shipwrecked on what was then an unknown island, they settled and subsequently named it Eleutheros, the Greek word meaning freedom and the basis for Eleuthera, as it is now called. However, religious differences and difficulties in establishing plantations disillusioned the colonists, some of whom returned to their homeland. Later on, in 1670, the islands were granted by King Charles II of England to the Lords Proprietors of South Carolina, who set up a loose form of personal legislature to rule their desolate territory.

The city of Nassau was originally a township known as Charles Town, named for King Charles II of England. Nicholas Trott, a proprietary governor of The Bahamas from 1694 to 1700, laid

---

26 P. Albury, *The Story of The Bahamas,* London & Basingstoke, Macmillan Press, Ltd., 1975, p. 38.

out Charles Town in 1695 and renamed it Nassau in honour of the Prince of Orange-Nassau who became King William III of England. At that time Nassau was a town comprising 160 houses, two public buildings, and a single church.[27] To these Governor Trott added a fort which he named Fort Nassau, located on the harbour site which is now the location of the British Colonial Hilton Hotel.

The development of economic activity in the early years of Bahamian history relied on a variety of commercial enterprises both legal and illegal. The period beginning near the end of the seventeenth and continuing well into the eighteenth century was called the Golden Age of Piracy. Well-known pirates such as Henry Jennings, Sir Francis Drake, Blackbeard (Edward Teach), and many other famous pirates and privateers used the Bahamian islands as a base. The many islands and cays with channels and dangerous shoals provided numerous hiding places for pirate ships near busy merchant shipping lanes. When The Bahamas became an official British colony in 1717, a former English privateer, Woodes Rogers, became the first royal governor of The Bahamas.

Rogers served two terms as governor, during which he successfully drove off Spanish invaders and expelled from the colony all known pirates, including Calico Jack (John Rackham), Anne Bonny, and Mary Reade, who were later captured in Jamaica. This insured a climate for the slow development of trade, and inspired the former national motto of the country: *Expulsis piratis restituta commercia* (Pirates expelled commerce restored). He is today memorialized by a life-sized statue at the front entrance of the British Colonial Hilton Hotel as well as a street along the city waterfront now known commonly as the Market Range, but officially named Woodes Rogers Wharf.

27 P. Albury, pp. 53–54.

During the Seven Years' War between England and France, which began in 1756, privateering regained the popularity it enjoyed during the late seventeenth century. This infamous activity, wherein a government authorizes the use of a ship that belongs to a private entity to engage in battle, became very prevalent and profitable for many ship owners and seamen. Nassau became the main base. Accordingly, as a defensive measure, very substantial fortifications were built or restored at prominent hilltops in order to guard the entrances to the harbour. Fort Charlotte, built in 1789 on the hilltop overlooking Arawak Cay and the entrance to the harbor, is one remaining example. This period, though turbulent, saw great wealth and prosperity but was followed by many years of economic hardship at the end of the Seven Years' War.

During the American War of Independence the colony once again prospered as a base for privateers who preyed on the shipping trade between the American rebel colonies and their Spanish allies in Cuba. Indeed, the Spaniards eventually occupied New Providence for almost a year until they were ousted by the British.

The formal ending of the war against the North American colonies, ratified by the Treaty of Versailles of 1782, also had an economic effect on The Bahamas. Following the treaty, many thousands of loyalists from the southern states of America who wished to maintain their English connection moved to several of the islands across The Bahamas including New Providence, Abaco, Exuma, Eleuthera, Cat Island, and Watlings Island. They obtained crown grants from the British government in order to re-establish their homes, farmlands, and other developments and brought their slaves with them, maintaining the plantation system. As a result, by the end of the eighteenth century the population of The Bahamas had doubled to approximately 9,000, two-thirds of which were the descendants of former African slaves. This changed the social, economic, and political landscape of The

Bahamas, whereby prejudicial racial lines were set down and followed for centuries to come.

With the influx of the loyalists from the United States between 1783 and 1785, the economy in the colony soon drastically improved. The immigrants introduced cotton production on a plantation scale in 1784 and also extended commercial agriculture. Although the profits realized from the large cotton crops were occasionally ruined by the infestation of insects, the industry was the mainstay of the economy.

Shipwrecking soon followed cotton growing as a profitable source of income. As a result of this illegal enterprise, whereby local seamen deliberately misplaced buoys and other markers, ships entering or transshipping through Bahamian waters were intentionally misguided onto dangerous reefs and shoals and became hopelessly stranded or wrecked. The perpetrators of these deliberately caused shipwrecks would then enrich themselves from the resulting floating cargo and treasure. This profitable means of revenue was further enhanced by privateering, which yet again became extremely popular and profitable, especially during the French Revolution of 1789–1799 and the American War of 1812, when many of the most outlandish pirates of the period became well-known historical figures for their daring and criminal buccaneering not only in Bahamian waters but throughout the Caribbean.

During the ensuing flourishing economic period of the late eighteenth and early nineteenth centuries, the American loyalists also permanently stamped an aspect of their culture on the islands, as they caused most of the existing and impressive historic buildings and statues to be erected in Nassau, displaying the architecture of the period. Local enactments now exist that are designed to preserve and prevent any further deterioration of these existing buildings.

On August 28, 1833, the British passed the Slavery Abolition Act, and although there was a requirement for the freed slaves to undergo a four-year period of apprenticeship, they all became fully free in 1838. The first Monday in August is today still observed as a legal holiday celebrating the emancipation of slaves that took place on August 1, 1834. The liberated black population of The Bahamas then outnumbered the white population three to one and they soon established settlements across New Providence Island, outside the city boundaries of Nassau, which was primarily occupied by the white population.

New Providence, while only twenty-one miles long from east to west, and seven miles from north to south at its widest point, has always been the most populated district in the chain of islands. Along most of the island's length from east to west, there run two prominent hill ranges. One range runs fairly close to the northern shoreline, and it is this sea-front coastal area, extending from the northern coast to the hilltop, that was occupied and developed by the first settlers who lived on New Providence and developed the capital city, Nassau, on that site.

Apart from being the business and civic hub of the island, the city of Nassau was also the main residential area of the white and mulatto population, as well as home to the middle-class minority comprising the racially mixed and most of the then affluent coloured population. As the population grew, these city dwellers correspondingly extended their residences eastwards and westwards from the city limits, along or near the northern waterfront of the island, but never southwards over the hill ridge.

Many small communities populated by black residents, however, were developed south of the Governor's residence in areas dubbed "Over the Hill," including Grant's Town and Bain Town; others settled in more distant areas such as Gambier, Fox Hill, Carmichael, and Adelaide Village.

The story of Over the Hill is in itself the history of a proud and aspiring segment of the Bahamian people. It is the story of freed slaves who had been forcibly taken from their native land in West Africa and settled in a new land across the Atlantic Ocean. It is a story of the preservation of many aspects of an ancient culture, combined with the acquisition of modern skills and quality education, in order to achieve success in a new land.

Grant's Town was once the mecca of future leaders, builders, educators, politicians, and business and professional people, as well as ordinary artisans and workers, all of whom lived there and developed the area as they established a fine record of black families and proud neighborhoods. Sadly, that reputation has changed in recent decades, as Over the Hill is now fast becoming a symbol of the deterioration of those very same neighborhoods due to overpopulation and poor property maintenance.

Almost in the center of this hilltop area and forming the southern limits of the city is a higher area which became known as Mount Fitzwilliam. This area was acquired by the government of the day to establish the official residence and office of the governor of the colony at that time, the Honourable Richard Fitzwilliam, governor of The Bahamas from 1733 to 1740.

For the most part, the residents of "ova-da-hill," as it was (and still often is) pronounced, remained generally docile and subservient to the folks uptown on whom they relied for their meager income. Indeed, during the colony's annual tourist season, which was then only in the winter months, visitors would sometimes be taken on tours of Grant's Town—to see "the native section."

And so it was in those early days that if you lived or hailed from an area like Grant's Town, you were not only discriminated against as a black or coloured person, but you were also underprivileged, and stamped automatically with a badge of social inferiority and subservience. Hence, one frequently was dismissed with the rhetorical condemnation, adapted from the age-old biblical question, "Can any good thing come out of Grant's Town?"

The business establishments of the day were all located to the north of the hill range, providing a natural southern and protective boundary to the city limits. Official buildings—starting with Government House, as well as the city's only bank at the time, the government offices, the commercial shops, professional offices, the electrical power plant and public works department—were all located north of the hill, and primarily along Bay Street.

Over the Hill was not an economically vibrant neighbourhood, but those residents who were not permanently employed "out town," meaning in the Nassau city limits, or were not tradesmen or mechanics, were usually innovative in making a living as streetside or itinerant vendors. Fish vendors purchased their supplies from the main fish market on Bay Street or from nearby sloops moored west of the Prince George dock. In the same way, some enterprising women would walk through the district carrying large trays of vegetables on their heads, making daily sales to house-owners who had not gone out to the market. Others carried on their heads huge bundles of dried grass, tied in a bed sheet, as they moved through the neighborhood shouting "Bed grass! Bed grass!" which was regularly purchased by those who could not afford regular mattresses and so utilized this native material to make homemade pads for their beds.

The entrepreneurial spirit was even prevalent among the youth. Teenage boys, for example, went through the area every evening delivering newspapers to their subscribers, or making sales to customers on the street.

The education system in The Bahamas was at that time negligible, especially for those residents who were descendants of former slaves; however, the government established two central public schools which were fed by preparatory schools operated primarily by churches.

The constitutional rights of black Bahamians were also limited in areas such as the right to vote, qualification to sit as jurors, and most especially the numerous instances in which the practice of discrimination was a way of life with a de facto apartheid in place. In fact, prior to 1956, when an antidiscrimination resolution was passed in the House of Assembly, the black population was not allowed to enter hotels and clubs, some movie theatres and schools, and even the front areas of certain churches, let alone live in the white districts on the northern coastline.

Over the Hill, therefore, was more than a geographic description, it was also a concept, an identity, a heritage, and a way of life. First developed as a hybrid of African and European traditions and customs, Bahamian culture has likewise been greatly affected by the influence of American tourism, especially the music and dress introduced by the many visitors.

Quite apart from the population growth in Nassau and across New Providence, settlements had been established over the years on many of the other islands in the Bahamian group, each of which embraced the history and culture which was common to all. But at the same time each had its own distinctive and colorful industry and special features. Most of these islands, formerly called the Out Islands and now known as the Family Islands, developed thriving industries during the nineteenth and early twentieth centuries, and were individually known for their particular products and customs. Collectively, all of the islands in the chain provide both a happy contrast and at the same time a wonderfully interlocking compatibility with one another.

As indicated in the Preface, one of the goals of this book is to intertwine the unique history and geography of the islands with the history and legacy of one unique man. It seems appropriate, then, to discuss in a bit more detail the territory the Duke was sent to govern.

GRAND BAHAMA, in the northernmost area of the Bahamian archipelago, is the fourth-largest and now the second most populated and economically strong island. Its modern city of Freeport was established in 1955 by Wallace Groves, an American financier who built the resort city of Lucaya and attracted investors to the island to take advantage of its many attractions and tax-free status. As a result, the early settlers who made a living both fishing and harvesting the abundant timber from the vast pine forests on the island for the most part abandoned their land and trades to join an economic boom which flowed from the large increase in tourism.

Just south of Grand Bahama, lying a mere forty miles east of the city of Miami, Florida, are the two small islands comprising NORTH BIMINI and SOUTH BIMINI. These western islands in The Bahamas became infamous in the 1920s during the Era of Prohibition in the United States when the shores of Bimini were used for the bootlegging and rum-running of liquor into America at a period when the United States was known as "Dry America." Bimini has also acquired historical fame as the location of the mythic Fountain of Youth, as well as the site of the fabled Lost City of Atlantis in the shallow waters off its shores. In fact present-day divers still claim to observe in the clear waters the symmetrical slabs known as the Bimini Stones, which are supposedly the paving stones of the road leading into the legendary Atlantis. Today, Bimini is still world-famous for its annual big-game fishing tournaments, and North Bimini is currently undergoing the development of a huge tourist project known as Bimini Bay Resort and Casino.

The second-largest island, ABACO, part of a group of islands to the north and east of Grand Bahama, is inhabited by an industrious population, which became well known for exporting timber, pineapples, sisal, and fish. Many of its residents have developed boatbuilding as a specialty, which became a major enterprise for many of its residents until recent years; big-game fishing is also popular in the area.

Immediately southwest of Abaco, the BERRY ISLANDS are likewise a chain made up of about thirty islands and in excess of a hundred cays, sometimes referred to as the fish bowl of The Bahamas. With a population of well under 1,000, these islands were settled in 1836 by a group of freed slaves but remained relatively undeveloped; however, during the winter season they are visited by out-of-town guests and second-home residents with the main attraction being big-game fishing and scuba diving.

ANDROS is the largest island in The Bahamas and is a natural wonderland with its inland freshwater lakes, wildlife, pine forests, and creeks, as well as a huge and expansive concentration of mangroves. Andros boasts the third-largest barrier reef in the world, following Australia and Belize, and its waters include a rare geologic blue hole. It is the nearest island to New Providence, lying just twenty miles to the west. Although most of the island is undeveloped, it holds the well-known site of the U.S. Navy's Atlantic Undersea Test and Evaluation Center (AUTEC). Prior to being scourged by a devastating virus, sponging was once a flourishing industry on the island, together with many plantations of cotton, sisal, sugar cane, and other crops. The island does have a long history of boatbuilding, straw work, and wood-carving, but it is perhaps best known today for the development of a colorful batik fabric and clothing manufacturing enterprise called Androsia, sold on almost all of the inhabited islands of The Bahamas since 1973, and also now enjoying success as a quality export fabric product that is regarded as truly Bahamian in both design and spirit.

ELEUTHERA and HARBOUR ISLAND are famous, respectively, for their pineapple plantations and pink sand beaches. These islands, located to the east of New Providence, were settled in the 1700s by British loyalists who influenced a style of architecture and way of life which has since been adopted by other Bahamian islands. Indeed, Harbour Island has been ranked by travel specialists as one of the best islands in the Caribbean. These islands are home to upwards of 10,000 residents who, as they have for centuries, either fish or farm for their livelihood.

Immediately to the south of Eleuthera is CAT ISLAND, which is the sixth-largest in the chain of islands. It boasts the nation's highest point, Mount Alvernia, also known as Como Hill, which rises to a height of 206 feet, impressive for an island nation, where it is topped by a monastery called The Hermitage, a group of buildings erected by a Franciscan monk, Brother Jerome Hawes, in the 1940s. In earlier years Cat Island farmers gained wealth primarily from their cotton plantations; one of their main economic crops today is the cascarilla bark, which is exported to Italy to provide the main ingredient in the liqueur Campari as well as certain medicines and scents. Sir Sidney Poitier, the Academy Award–winning actor, best-selling author, and arguably one of the world's most famous Bahamians, was raised in Arthur's Town on the northwest side of the island. A new bridge between Nassau and Paradise Island has recently been named in his honour with much celebration and fanfare.

More or less in the middle of the Bahamian chain, the district of EXUMA consists of over 360 small islands and cays, the largest of which is known as Great Exuma, which is joined by a small bridge to its smaller island called Little Exuma. Settled by American loyalists who left the American mainland after the Revolutionary War of 1776, the expatriates established a cotton-plantation economy, which has gradually been replaced by tourist-related trades. One of these loyalist settlers was Baron John Rolle, who upon his death in 1842 bequeathed all of his large landholdings in Exuma to his slaves; as a result two of its major towns today are known as Rolle Town and Rolleville. The main settlement, George Town, was named in honour of King George III of England. Since 2000, as a result of the construction of resort properties and direct flights from the United States and Canada, the population of Exuma has more than doubled. Tourism and marine-related sports sustain a large portion of the island's economy.

SAN SALVADOR, still bearing its Spanish name after Christ the Saviour, is celebrated for its historical reputation as the first landing site of Christopher Columbus during his first expedition to the New World, arriving at its shores on October 12, 1492. Apart from its historic significance, today the island enjoys a strong tourist industry due primarily to its many sandy beaches, reefs for scuba diving, and resort facilities, as well as a research centre where in excess of 1,000 researchers and students are involved annually in studies of marine geology, biology, and archaeology.

RUM CAY to the southwest has a similar historical background as its neighbor. Although there is no extant record of Columbus actually landing in San Salvador, there is written documentation that a day later, on October 13, he did go ashore on the nearby island, Santa Maria de la Concepción, now called Rum Cay, a mere twenty-odd miles away. Rumor has it that the island received its new name because a ship wrecked on one of its surrounding reefs, spilling barrels and barrels of rum that washed up on its shores.

In the past the island exported salt, sisal, and pineapples. However, much of this economic activity was overridden by competition for its pineapples from neighboring islands and even the distant Hawaiian Islands, as well as the devastation to its salt flats caused by destructive storms. The island holds the distinction of being the birthplace of Sir Milo B. Butler, the first Bahamian governor general of an independent Bahamas.

Although the population of Bahamian residents is small, the island now attracts vacation-home owners from many countries because of its undeveloped natural beauty on both land and sea, including a pristine coral reef for snorkeling and scuba diving.

LONG ISLAND, to the west, has the reputation of being the most scenic island in the Bahamian chain. The island is geographically famous for being divided by the Tropic of Cancer. It is particularly noted for its steep, rocky headlands, caves, and the famed Dean's Blue Hole, with a depth of 202 metres (663 ft.), being the world's deepest underwater sinkhole by almost double other known holes. Almost two centuries ago, Long Island was the site of an unfortunate incident at sea when a Swedish ship capsized, leaving two brothers with the surname Tornquist stranded in the ocean. Although both were rescued, one brother later returned to his home in Kalmar, Sweden, while the other remained and established himself as a planter in the settlement of Deadman's Cay. He was naturalized as a British subject in 1819 and married Mary Darville of Long Island. The couple raised three children, Charles William Tornquist, Mary Elizabeth Tornquist, and John Robertson Tornquist, who was the great-great-grandfather of the author. Over the years the spelling of the surname has been anglicized to Turnquest, and today the Turnquests are a well-known Bahamian family residing mainly on Long Island and New Providence.

Just below Long Island to the southeast are ACKLINS, CROOKED ISLAND, and LONG CAY, a rural group of small islands that are very popular with visiting fishermen and yachtsmen, and are world-famous for their display of naturally beautiful landscape, comprising white sandy beaches and private resorts.

RAGGED ISLAND, although never known for a vibrant tourist industry, has a proud and interesting history. Like Rum Cay, it developed a prosperous salt industry, exporting this product to Cuba and Haiti. Its only settlement on the island, Duncan Town, was named after Duncan Taylor, who operated its salt ponds. These suffered considerable hurricane damage in the 1950s; today its small population engages mainly in bone fishing and crawfishing.

The most easterly island in the Bahamian chain is MAYAGUANA, one of the few Bahamian islands which has retained its Lucayan name. Bordered on its eastern shores by the deep waters of the Atlantic Ocean, it is the most isolated Bahamian island, with a population of just over 300. It is known for its fertile soil, good farming, and its woody terrain.

In the southernmost part of The Bahamas is INAGUA, actually comprised of two islands known as Great Inagua and Little Inagua and named for the herbivorous iguana which is a native to its shores. It is the third largest in the Bahamian chain and is today almost entirely involved in the production of salt by the Morton Salt Company. Eighty salt ponds, covering over 12,000 acres of the two islands, produce almost one million pounds of salt annually for processing and export around the world. In addition, Inagua National Park, comprising some 287 square miles, is home to the world's largest colonies of flamingoes numbering in excess of 60,000. Legend claims that upon Henry Christophe's establishing himself as king of nearby Haiti in the late eighteenth century, he built a summer palace for himself on Inagua, but no traces of it can be found today.

Although the United States was central to tourism for the islands of The Bahamas throughout the twentieth century, and continues to provide the main source of tourists visiting The Bahamas into the twenty-first century, the Bahamian nation has also been the unintended recipient of both prosperity and financial difficulties resulting from U.S. laws. As it did worldwide, World War I brought hardship to the colony as a whole, but particularly affected the Out Islands, where work was practically nonexistent, resulting in a scarcity of food and other provisions. This hardship was, however, soon alleviated as a result of the Eighteenth Amendment passed by the United States Congress in December 1919 prohibiting the manufacture, importation, and sale of intoxicating liquor. The proximity of The Bahamas to the American mainland by sea enabled the smuggling of liquor into the United States, benefitting the many Bahamian merchants who engaged in an industry that between 1919 and 1923 became the most lucrative (albeit illegal) business in the history of the colony. Despite bringing a measure of comparative prosperity to the colony, the main profits flowed to only a few. When the United States repealed the Prohibition Act, the negative effect on the colony's economy was immediately felt. It was not until a decade later, after the outbreak of World War II, that other factors enabled a turnaround in the economic depression which had set in.

The British government selected the western section of New Providence to establish a Royal Air Force base. For this purpose a larger airport was built, providing much employment and giving a beneficial boost to the colony's economy. This was accompanied by a further positive injection in the economy resulting from a contractual arrangement between the governments of the United States and The Bahamas, whereby Bahamian labourers were contracted to provide indentured farming on agricultural plantations in the United States, thereby enabling their young American farmers to be drafted into the U.S. armed forces.

On the other hand, U.S. laws have also had a negative impact on enterprises in The Bahamas. Agriculture has always been generally developed on small areas of land, with few exceptions like the cotton crop, because the irregular terrain does not allow the cultivation of wide areas of farmland. Farming has, therefore, remained largely a household industry with the majority of crops—primarily vegetables such as tomatoes, okra, and onions—being grown for the local market. Tomato farmers, however, were able to create a small yet sustainable industry by exporting their crops to the United States until tariffs and trade restrictions eliminated this major market for such produce. For example, the state of Florida imposed an embargo on tomatoes from The Bahamas in 1936, resulting in the loss of the farmers' only major buyers and thus their livelihood.

Banking has played an important role in the Bahamian economy from the twentieth century, generating one of the nation's principal sources of income. Banking is today the second-largest industry in The Bahamas after tourism. The first savings bank in the country was instituted by the government in 1836 and known as the Public Bank of The Bahamas. However, it collapsed in 1886, and a government savings bank was established in the same year under the control of the Post Office Department. Shortly thereafter, in 1889, The Bank of Nassau was opened, playing an important role in the commercial life of The Bahamas for nearly thirty years before it failed in 1916 due to mismanagement. In the meantime, banking services were also being provided by the Royal Bank of Canada beginning in 1908 when it first opened for business as the first foreign company to provide The Bahamas with first-rate banking services (and continues to this day to do so). After 1947, many other banks and trust companies opened in The Bahamas, including First National City Bank which began operation in 1960.

The government later established the Central Bank of The Bahamas, officially opened in 1974 by Her Majesty Queen Elizabeth II. The duties of the Central Bank of The Bahamas involve the oversight and regulation of the banking industry and advisement to financial institutions operating in The Bahamas. The international banking sector expanded and grew in the country in the years following World War II when international businesses discovered the advantage of financing international trade through institutions located in the tax-free environment of The Bahamas. This industry later expanded to encompass trust administration and estate planning for high-net-worth individuals interested in securing privacy around their business and wealth interests.

However diverse in race, national origin, wealth, or habitation among the many islands of the Bahamian archipelago, in January 1936 the loyal residents of what was then one of the smallest British colonies learned, like the rest of the world, of the death of King George V and of the accession to the throne of his eldest son, the bachelor Prince of Wales, who succeeded him as King Edward VIII. Bahamians were likewise stunned by the news that King Edward abdicated the throne in December 1936, a mere ten months into his rule, in order to marry Mrs. Wallis Simpson. However, it could not possibly have been imagined by anyone at the time, especially in The Bahamas, that these world-shaking events were soon to involve the history of the colony in a direct and significant way.

HIS ARRIVAL

In July of 1940 the former King Edward VIII, Duke of Windsor, was appointed governor of the Bahama Islands. It was on the tenth of July, 1940, that the *Nassau Daily Tribune*, one of two daily newspapers published in Nassau at the time, announced in a "stop press" on its front page: "Former King Appointed Governor of Bahamas." The related editorial in the same issue of that newspaper stated that the appointment of the Duke of Windsor as governor of The Bahamas was a surprise to the whole world, and went on to state that *The Times* in England, in referring to the appointment, described the office of governor of The Bahamas as one of the oldest and most honourable posts under the Crown.

The Duke unfortunately did not share this positive view about his appointment. Before even arriving to take up his post in The Bahamas, he had expressed keen disappointment, as revealed in a letter written to his London solicitor, George Allen, describing his feelings while he was on the voyage en route to "taking up this wretched appointment." He continued, saying that he viewed "the prospect of an indefinite period of exile on those Islands with profound gloom and despondency."[28]

Recently released private correspondence between the Duke and Winston Churchill shows that he still maintained that view nearly a year after his arrival. In a letter dated June 30, 1941, which he addressed to "My Dear Winston," he still bemoans his appointment; however he does concede the necessity for his being sent to the remote island chain. Referring to a letter from his brother the king, dated July 26, 1940, he says it "leaves no doubt in my mind but that my banishment to these Islands was as good a war time expedience for a hopeless and insoluble situation as could be found."[29]

Sailing from Spain via Bermuda aboard the *Lady Somers*, the Duke and Duchess landed at the Prince George dock in central Nassau on August 17, 1940. The landing ceremony was a colourful occasion and, for at least the colony and its residents, a most historic event. The Duke and Duchess were greeted by members of the Governor's Executive Council, the highest decision-making body in the land. They accompanied the royal couple across Bay Street, past the impressive statue of Queen Victoria erected in Rawson Square, directly in front of the ancient House of Assembly, and into the Legislative Council building, which housed the upper chamber. It was there that Sir Oscar Bedford Daly, chief justice of The Bahamas, performed the swearing-in ceremony of the new governor and commander in chief, who thereupon officially assumed the governorship of the colony.

In light of present-day perceptions, however, the official welcoming reception, though appropriately ceremonial, was marred

---

28 M. Bloch, *The Duchess of Windsor,* New York, St. Martin's Press, 1996, p. 101.

29 Higham, p. 321.

by the racial and social status quo which was the prevailing and accepted state of affairs in the 1940s. Despite an eighty-five-percent black majority in the Bahamian population, no black individual sat on the Governor's Executive Council or served in any of the official positions of governance. The seats in the country's Legislative Council, whose members were appointed by the governor, and its House of Assembly, whose members were elected by "qualified" males, were both overwhelmingly occupied by whites.

It was therefore not surprising that all the arrangements for the welcoming program in Rawson Square included only white officials and their wives and other prominent individuals in the white community. Indeed, even the welcome bouquet of flowers for the Duchess was presented to her by an endearing little white toddler, Sonia Duncombe, today the wife of a former pre-independence cabinet minister and a successful practising barrister, the Honourable Godfrey Kelly, who has recently retired as senior partner of the law firm of Higgs & Kelly.

Upon learning of the Duke's appointment, Dr. C. R. Walker, who was then a leading representative of the Over the Hill black community, forwarded a proposal to the Governor's Executive Council suggesting a community-wide welcome celebration to be held on the spacious parade grounds of Clifford Park. Located at the foot of Fort Charlotte, the park had been developed during the administration of Sir Bede Clifford, for whom it was named. Dr. Walker's request was considered by the council at a meeting held on August 15, 1940, presided over by the colonial secretary, the Honourable W. L. Heape, who was acting governor in the interim between the departure of Sir Charles Dundas and the arrival of the Duke.

The council objected. Rather than accede to this reasonable request, they informed Dr. Walker that his proposition was being delayed in order for his request to be submitted for the approval of His Royal Highness. At the first meeting of the council over which the Duke presided, he did indeed approve the welcome ceremony to be held at Clifford Park on Friday, August 23, five days after his arrival.

The black community turned out in thousands to welcome the new royal governor. For hours before the time fixed for the commencement of the proceedings, the main thoroughfares leading to Clifford Park were congested with uniformed groups of marching Boy Scouts and Friendly Societies, all bearing their colourful banners and competing for space on the roadways as they approached the site of the celebration. The crowd gathered throughout the entire area of historic Fort Charlotte, which surrounded the decorated parade grounds of Clifford Park. The Guard of Honour, comprising all the uniformed groups in attendance, presented a picturesque support group for the platform guests—senior officials and leaders of the various political, social, and commercial units of the colony.

A notable welcoming program was presented by a group of local black leaders including Dr. C. R. Walker, Milo Butler, L. W. Young, S. C. McPherson, Rev. W. V. Eneas, and Bert Cambridge. Arguably the most memorable event of the day, however, was the presentation of flowers by a group of young Bahamian girls, including Phillipa (Bethell) Grant, Vernita Butler, Grace Wilson, Diana Johnson, Inez Johnson, Audrey Wilson, Sylvia Rhodriquez, Cyprianna (Bethel) Fleischer, Edna Logan, Delores Cambridge, Yvonne North, and Carolyn (Williams) Bartlett.[30]

The ceremony concluded with a speech by E. R. Bain welcoming the Duke and Duchess and committing the people of The Bahamas to work for the public good, for the Empire, and for the

30 E. Dupuch, "Welcome to Duke and Duchess of Windsor," *Nassau Daily Tribune*, 24 August 1940.

betterment of mankind. In his response the Duke thanked him and the entire committee and promised interest and support on new ventures to enhance the prosperity of the Bahama Islands, adding that he would not exclude the Out Islands and would visit them in due course.

Although these various events represented a festive and ceremonial welcome to The Bahamas, having officially assumed his post as governor and commander in chief the Duke assiduously set about the task of governance. In this capacity he presided over the regular meetings of the Executive Council, which constitutionally directed the government of the country. The Duchess likewise set upon fulfilling her various duties as First Lady and with the task of renovating Government House, the official governor's residence which the Duke and Duchess found completely unbefitting as their living quarters.

GOVERNMENT HOUSE

One of the most famous sites in The Bahamas is Government House on Mount Fitzwilliam at the top of George Street in the city of Nassau. It has been the official habitation of all the governors of The Bahamas since 1801. It was in this imposing and historic old building that the royal couple took up residence after a short official welcoming ceremony at Prince George Wharf. Notwithstanding the historic sentiment attached to Government House, the Duchess was not impressed.

Before she even arrived in The Bahamas, the Duchess had already formed a negative opinion of their intended official residence. In a letter she wrote to her Aunt Bessie on August 7, 1940, while en route to the island nation, she bemoans the condition of Government House, stating, "I have awful reports of the house— small, hideous, hardly any furniture—all unsatisfactory."[31]

31 Bloch, p. 103.

Without a doubt, the Duke and Duchess found the accommodations at their official residence both inadequate for their needs
and lacking in sufficient opulence for their taste and status. The
Duke acted quickly to address the issue of suitable living quarters. The Windsors moved out of Government House after only
one week, and at a meeting just one month after he took office, he
proposed that the building be renovated. The council agreed to an
expenditure of £5,000, which was to be in addition to £2,000 previously authorized for the renovation and repair of Government
House. In 1940, the pound was worth around US $4.00.

For temporary quarters, the Windsors moved into a palatial residence on Prospect Ridge owned by Frederick Sigrist, the British
millionaire designer of the Hawker aircraft known as the Spit-
fire, which later achieved notoriety for its effective use by the RAF
during the Battle of Britain in the critical years of World War
II. In 1940 the Sigrists were longtime residents of The Bahamas,
and spent their summers abroad. That November, when they
returned to Nassau for their winter stay, the Windsors again
relocated, taking up residence at Westbourne, the Cable Beach
country mansion of Sir Harry Oakes, who offered them the use
of this property until the renovations at Government House were
completed. Although Sir Harry was one of the wealthiest men in
the world, and Westbourne certainly was appropriate for a man
of his affluence, the Duchess nevertheless disdainfully described it
as "a shack by the sea."[32]

Given the royal couple's lofty standards, the rebuilding work
and the redecoration at Government House, not surprisingly, were
extensive. In addition to the expenditure by the government, the
Duchess herself supervised the interior decoration with the assistance of a professional designer out of New York. She brought in

32 Bloch, p. 144.

exquisite period pieces of French furniture as well as other articles befitting a royal princess.

The renovations to Government House were completed during the early months of 1941, whereupon the new royal governor and his wife moved into the official residence and the Duke settled in quickly to the task of governance of this small colony.

It is worthy of note that in 1995, more than half a century after these improvements were made, the present author, on becoming governor general, was responsible for organizing the only complete major renovations and refurbishing to be carried out to all areas of Government House since the repairs effected for the Windsors.

Government House was originally erected on a site purchased by the Crown in 1800 for the sum of £4,000. This ten-acre city block, and the property and former building thereon, had originally been rented as the residence of successive governors since 1737. As noted earlier, Mount Fitzwilliam is named after Sir Richard Fitzwilliam, a former owner of the site, who succeeded Woodes Rogers as governor from 1733 to 1738.

The construction of the residence itself took place in 1801, one year after the White House in Washington was built. The eastern wing was added in 1907 to house the grand ballroom on the upper floor, and the offices of the governor and his staff downstairs. This eastern wing was badly damaged during a hurricane and replaced by a new structure in 1909. As a result of the devastating hurricane of 1929, when the main house suffered substantial damage as well, the present structure was rebuilt maintaining the original solid outside walls; the interior and front façade were entirely redesigned, with the present colonial columns added to the main entrance.

The upstairs living quarters of the house are arranged along both sides of a wide, high-ceilinged hall leading from the grand

staircase. On the southern side of the hallway is the large master
bedroom which during the Duke's occupancy doubled as his bedroom and private study. Across the hall is a suite of three rooms
which to this day is called the Duchess of Windsor Suite; it com-
prises a sitting room, bathroom, bedroom, and study. In addition,
there are three large guest bedroom suites, two of which have their
own sitting room and an enclosed verandah overlooking the expansive, lovely gardens to the south. At the western end of the great
hall there is a large breakfast room, which also serves as a private
sitting room. Downstairs are the formal state rooms, including an
elegant, tastefully decorated large drawing room; across the hall
is another sitting room which doubles as a library, and this opens
into the large state dining room with its historic 26-place dining
table made of Honduran mahogany specially imported for fabri-
cation by local craftsmen and now almost a century old. Serving
the dining room is a butler's pantry and the maid's pantry, both of
which adjoin a large kitchen and storerooms.

To all of this, after the Duke's arrival in 1940, a new three-story
west wing was added to house four guest suites to accommodate
his personal staff, with a large sitting room which today serves as a
library. The two lower floors are utilized as staff and maintenance
offices, accommodation for security officers, laundry facilities, and
storerooms. It is still known today as the Windsor Wing.

As part of the refurbishment implemented for the Duke and
his Duchess, a window air-conditioning unit was installed in each
of the major rooms of the residence and the new west wing. This
remained the form of interior climate control to the residence until
1995 when the present author, who was appointed governor general in that year, procured governmental approval for the installation of central air-conditioning throughout the entire property,
including the ballroom and offices, as part of an overall renovation process.

Many items of furniture originally brought in by the Duchess are still in place today, including several pieces which had to be restored, but all of which provide testimony to the style and quality of the regal and dignified furnishing which the Duchess carried out. Some of the pieces are worthy of special note. In the foyer to the main entrance there is a magnificent mirror, very ornate in its gilded border, which provides a talking piece to every visitor.

Another special feature is the superb oak door at the front entrance of Government House, which has quite a history of its own, believed to have been designed and fabricated in Wales and presented to the Duke when he was inducted as Prince of Wales, for installation at the entrance to his personal bachelor's apartments in Buckingham Palace. The legend continues that he arranged for the door to be reinstalled at the front entrance of each of his later residences, and eventually had it placed at the front entrance to Government House shortly after he arrived in The Bahamas.

At the completion of his term as governor, at the end of World War II, the Duke was very engaged in winding up his personal affairs and also in his efforts to seek a further and more significant appointment as an ambassador to the United States or as governor general of Canada.[33] In the meantime, the Duchess had already left The Bahamas to live at her family's place of origin in Baltimore until he could join her. As the story now goes, in the Duke's haste to leave The Bahamas, he made no arrangements for the door to be dismantled and sent to him, and it has remained in place ever since.

Notwithstanding its real or legendary history, what certainly is fact is that an examination of the door discloses three or four very

33 Duke of Windsor to Sir John Stephens, *Colonial Office Papers CO23/785*, 21 June 1945.

visible impressions, in different but close proximity to each other, disclosing where hinges had previously held the door in its different frames at different periods.

The present main feature of the door is its upper panel, the timber of which has been removed to encase a glass pane on which is emblazoned, in gold leaf, the crest and coat of arms of the Order of the Garter into which the Duke was installed as a member on his sixteenth birthday, when he officially became the Prince of Wales.

Now a permanent part of the entrance to Government House, this regal relic depicts a carved and gilded crown sitting atop a gilded hexagonal badge within the centre of which is inscribed a large hexagonal-shaped letter "E" and the motto of the Order of the Garter:

Honi soit qui mal y pense.

"Shame on him who thinks evil."

PART 2

HIS TENURE

GOVERNMENT AND
THE LEADERS

Englishmen who founded colonies in various parts of the world carried with them their parliamentary practices and procedures; however, for all practical purposes, these colonies conducted their own governmental affairs. Because of the lack of speedy transportation and efficient communications, the government of Westminster routinely gave these settlers a liberal form of government, reserving for the Crown only executive authority and power.

In the early eighteenth century, Captain Woodes Rogers came to The Bahamas as the colony's first royal governor. He introduced the historic and long-standing constitution of 1729, establishing one of the oldest parliaments in the British family of nations. The Bahamas House of Assembly yields pride of tradition only to the British House of Commons, the "mother of parliaments," from which it sprang. It is interesting that the present mace, the emblem of authority of the Speaker in the House of Assembly in The Bahamas, was made in England in 1799.

The Bahamas legislature was similar in form and procedure to that of the colonies on the American mainland prior
to the War of Independence. As the years went by, when government became more complex and new problems arose, intervention by England in local affairs created areas of conflict, and
the sturdy, independence-minded colonists fought to preserve
what they considered were the rights and privileges of their own
parliaments.

As a result, The Bahamas, Barbados, and Bermuda came to
be known as "The Three Bs" because each carried a sting that
often barbed deep into any attempts at over-lordship by England's
Colonial Office. Substantively, however, the government of The
Bahamas was patterned after that of Great Britain.

The governor, on appointment, became the representative head
of state. He was also the commander in chief "in and over the
Bahama Islands and the official representative of the sovereign."
The governor was appointed by the Crown. His term of office was
usually three years but could be extended at the discretion of the
sovereign on the advice of the Colonial Office.

The executive branch of government, over which the governor
presided, took the form of and was called the Executive Council.
The colonial secretary, the attorney general, and the receiver general and treasurer were the three ex-officio members of this high
forum, with six additional unofficial members appointed locally
by the Colonial Office on the recommendation of the governor,
with their appointment being issued by the sovereign's commission. Unofficial members were normally appointed for a five-year
term, but limited to two terms.

The legislative branch consisted of the Legislative Council,
comparable to the House of Lords in England, except that it
had more power than its British counterpart. There was also
the House of Assembly, similar to the House of Commons in

England, in that it was an elected body. Members of the Legislative Council were appointed for ten-year periods, with two possible reappointments of five years each. Members of the House were elected for a seven-year period by various electoral districts throughout the colony. A general election was held every seven years, with by-elections being held whenever a vacancy arose through resignation, death, or appointment of a member to the Legislative Council. A man could be a member of both the House of Assembly and the Executive Council at the same time. Parties did not come to the political life of The Bahamas until 1956, when the first political party, the Progressive Liberal Party, was formed.

The legislature has always followed the same forms and ceremonies as the "mother of parliaments," the procedure being based on Erskine May's *Parliamentary Practice* with modifications as set out in the *Manual of Cabinet and Ministry Procedure* of the House of Assembly.

Under this political system, which the Duke of Windsor found operating in full force when he arrived in The Bahamas to assume executive command of The Bahamas in 1940, the Houses of Parliament exercised complete control over the finances of the colony. They alone could introduce financial legislation and impose taxation, and they rejected any claims by the Legislative Council to such rights to amend a money measure. With its legislative background of more than two centuries of experience, the House knew well how to get legislation passed that would otherwise not be countenanced by the Legislative Council or the governor. The House would often introduce additional provisions attached to urgent financial measures; since the Legislative Council could not disallow such money measures outright, their only recourse was to pass it under protest. Therein lay the real power of the House.

This monetary power vested in the House was also shown through another phase of government. The governor could suggest but he could not force measures dealing with finance or taxation, his suggestions taking the form of a formal message to the House. The message was routinely sent to a House committee for consideration and to report back to the House; but this often became a tactical procedure whereby the governor's message or request for action might be indefinitely delayed and eventually allowed to die; if it were a measure the committee found appealing, however, it could take definite shape in a report to the House as a whole and would then be accepted as a product of the House.

The governor under this system did, however, have reserve powers over financial measures. No money could be paid out of the treasury without his warrant, and he could delay or refuse to issue that approval if he considered the colony's financial structure jeopardized by a vote of the House.

The Speaker, then as now, served as the presiding officer of the House, and was elected by members at the first meeting of a new session. He directed legislation through its various stages and ruled on points of procedure. No appeal could be brought against his rulings, but members could ask him to resign if they were strongly opposed to his stand. His powers and functions were almost identical with those of the Speaker of the House of Commons, with the one important difference: a Speaker in the colonies no longer has the power of arrest that is vested in the Speaker of the Commons. The point is, perhaps, academic, since the Speaker of the Commons no longer exercises this power. The Speaker puts all motions to the House, but does not himself vote unless there is a tie.

The governor was known as the "first gentleman" of the colony, and the Speaker as the "first commoner."

The functions of the president of the Legislative Council, appointed by the sovereign on the recommendation of the governor, were similar to those of the Speaker of the House. This post was regarded as the highest political appointment within the framework of the constitution. It was customarily followed by a knighthood.

Individual members of the Legislative Council, and of the House, had the right to introduce legislation, but most bills and measures in practice emanated from the executive branch of government, which was responsible for planning the conduct and management of the affairs of the colony.

The executive branch was represented in the House by five elected members, who were also appointed to the Executive Council. The senior member of this group was known as the leader for the government and he, with the support of his colleagues, introduced and spearheaded the executive program for the governance of the colony.

It was the Executive Council with which the Duke interacted, usually at weekly meetings, in seeking to carry out his administration of the colony. The official minutes of the Executive Council for the period of the Duke's tenure have disclosed many decisions he guided through that highest echelon of the government, providing the framework and the hallmark of his governance. Most interestingly, it was at his first meeting with the Council on August 21, 1940, that the governor-in-council decided to make an interest-free war loan to Britain of £250,000 (equivalent to US $1 million) from the colony's surplus funds.

In the early days of his term, the Duke felt that it was important to familiarize himself with all sections of this multi-island colonial jurisdiction, and not just the island of New Providence on which the capital city of Nassau stood. During the first several months after his arrival in Nassau, he visited many of the small, inhabited Out Islands.

The newly appointed governor also thoroughly acquainted himself with the constitutional and legislative structure of the local government, gaining necessary insight into the formalities required for him to successfully head the administration of an executive government for whose decisions and direction he would be solely responsible. He diligently applied himself to his job.

In short order he assessed the composition and abilities of his Council members, and shared his observations in a confidential letter written on July 26, 1941, to the Right Honorable Walter Moyne, who, as secretary of state for the colonies was the minister responsible for all British colonies, including The Bahamas, and who was therefore not only his "boss" but happened also to be a close friend.

In the letter, he bluntly disclosed what he thought of the governing team, stating that the "membership of the Council I have inherited in The Bahamas leaves much to be desired." Following are excerpts, expressing his largely negative opinions of the existing members, as he put it "from whom I at present officially seek advice."

The Hon. W. K. Moore, President of the Legislative Council:

"I was not going to recommend Mr. Moore for re-appointment and I am, in fact, considering persuading him to retire from the Presidency of the Upper House as he is old and as a result of sinus trouble is addicted to spells of activity of his right arm."

The Hon. A. K. Solomon, the present Government Leader in the House of Assembly:

". . . has unfortunately not the record of loyalty to his credit. The ablest and shrewdest of the older generation of Bahamian politicians, he has managed to create a powerful position for himself and although by no means a good lawyer, he has the best practice in Nassau where he has made a lot of money and is employed by all the rich winter residents and large owners of property by virtue of his local power and association with the Government. Mr. Solomon is the only consistently dissenting voice in Executive Council and while he is sly enough to fulfill his obligations as Government Leader by speaking in favour of messages sent by the Governor in Council and voting for legislation instigated from this source, he is not above lobbying against them beforehand if he disagrees, and even letting it be known both inside and outside the House of Assembly afterwards that what he had to say officially did not represent his personal viewpoint. These tactics are, of course, in flagrant violation of the conditions under which a man agrees to serve as Government Leader . . . "

The Hon. R. G. Collins:

"American born but became a Bahamian over thirty years ago. He is straighter than most of these politicians and is a useful and public-spirited citizen; and despite his age, works hard as Chairman of the Development board. Besides, he is a sick man and on top of this he had a bad motor accident a short while ago and his doctor has prescribed two months' rest from his Governmental duties, so that I do not know how long he is going to last. . . . I could be a lot worse off except for the fact that he is very inarticulate, which of course detracts from the value of his participation in debates."

The Hon. R. W. Sawyer:

"One of the outstanding crooks both politically and commercially and is universally mistrusted . . . it would be a great mistake to re-appoint him."

The Hon. H. G. Christie:

"A remarkable man having built up a big real estate business from nothing and, by faith that the future of these Islands lies in development by private enterprise, has had the vision to buy up large tracts of land both in New Providence and in the Out Islands, a great proportion of which he has succeeded in persuading wealthy Americans and others to buy. Although Mr. Christie is illiterate as well as inarticulate, and next to useless in the House of Assembly, he is, from contacts with big business in America and as a member of the Development Board, a useful link between my Council and foreign private enterprise, which is so valuable an element in The Bahamas."

The Duke concludes,

"From the above descriptions of my unofficial advisors, you will admit that they are not much of a team and unfortunately, the pool from which to choose future unofficial members of Executive Council is limited both in quantity and quality."[34]

Although the Duke's missive clearly shows his disdain for the Bahamian legislators, it likewise insightfully evaluates the social structure which existed in The Bahamas of that period. Moreover, his views are seen through the prism of the experienced eyes of one who not only worked with these legislators for a year, but who was also a world traveller who had an opportunity to meet and to weigh the worth and capabilities of men of ability and rank in many parts of the world.

In his analysis of the Council members, he explicitly describes

---

34 Bloch, p. 195.

in turn the character, abilities, and in some cases the perceived weaknesses of each of these leading citizens of the country. He also exhibits his priorities; although he found at least one member's contributions "useless," he nevertheless considered his connections in the foreign investment community as "useful" indeed.

More revealing, however, is the frank disclosure in this same letter that clearly shows his own racial bias on the "difficult problem" of colour prejudice in a community where the colour bar was strongly enforced. Although he writes that he personally did not hold very strong views one way or the other on the problem, and that while he does realize that it will have to be tackled sooner or later, he is quite sure that it is "a fence that must not be rushed" in The Bahamas. He states,

"After a year's experience of white Nassauvian mentality, any suggestion of the appointment of a coloured member to Executive Council would not only be unwelcome but meet with the utmost hostility, and while I, of course, see the advantages of such a gesture towards the coloured community, I am more than alive to its disadvantages.

"Finally, there is the social angle of the inclusion of the coloured element amongst the Governor's nominated advisors . . . were the coloured element to be introduced, the social colour bar would automatically be lifted. The coloured member of Executive Council and his wife would have to be invited to Government House on official occasions and it would undoubtedly follow that the coloured members of the Legislative Council and the House of Assembly would eventually expect to be invited with their wives to Government House as well."[35]

35 Bloch, p. 195.

The entire letter, written in confidence by the Duke to a high official in the British government, is a candid portrayal of his assessment of the Bahamian local leadership of the period; of his own prejudicial feelings, despite his protests to the contrary, with regard to the worth and dignity of human beings who were not white; of the weakness in his character by his stated unwillingness to make any moves that might be regarded as upsetting the status quo—and his stepping stone to more prestigious office; and of his obvious placement of value in those who could advance foreign investment in this colony over their capabilities to govern. It gives us a clear insight into what manner of man he—and his leaders—were.

THE PROJECT

As a result of the Japanese bombing on Pearl Harbor in December 1941, the United States was drawn into World War II. This resulted in an immediate collapse of the Bahamian tourism industry and caused serious unemployment throughout The Bahamas.

At the onset of the war an agreement between the British and American governments led to a number of military bases being built in several territories in the West Indies. One such location was New Providence, to be used as a base to train U.S. military airmen. On May 20, 1942, an American construction firm, Pleasantville Construction Corporation, began work on the airfield, an undertaking that become known as "the Project." In fact, two sites were developed: one was the existing small landing field that had been constructed by Sir Harry Oakes, then called Main Field but later renamed Oakes Field, and another called Satellite Field near the western end of the island in the Pine Barrens, which was also being developed as a military airfield.

The Bahamas was chosen for this military development because of its proximity to the United States and for its ideal climate. This airbase was intended to facilitate the training of airmen more quickly than the normal training period. Subsequently thousands of trainees were dispatched to both fields where they qualified in all aspects of air training before being posted to enter either the Pacific or European theatre of war.

The Pleasantville Construction Corporation brought in modern mechanical equipment with large quantities of building material to construct and complete the two airfields. They locally advertised extensively and hired some twenty-five hundred Bahamian labourers.

A contentious issue, however, was that the local labour gangs, entirely comprised of black men from Over the Hill and the Out Islands, were placed under the direction of two local white Bahamians. These men had convinced management that as former building contractors they would know best how to control the Bahamian workers; however, they not only failed to prevent the later uprising, which became known as the Burma Road Riot, but also fanned the flames of wide local unrest and discontent.

When news about the building project was publicized, and with the expectation of a lucrative employment opportunity, many men from the Out Islands flocked to New Providence to join the large number of workers who lived in the impoverished black communities of Grant's Town and Bain Town, East Street, McCullough Corner and Fort Hill, Mackey Street and Kemp Road, and Johnson Road and Fox Hill. The labourers from these areas were looking forward to the higher wages that foreign projects such as this one had historically brought.

It was also widely known that the workers from the United States were being paid around $3 a day and the local labourers fully expected the equivalent amount at the prevailing exchange rate, which would have been twelve shillings. The Bahamas was at that time still using the British currency, which continued until the establishment of the Bahamas Monetary Authority in 1968 and the conversion to dollars and cents, with the Bahamian dollar being equivalent in value to the U.S. dollar.

The Bahamian workers had two main concerns: the inadequacy of pay and the fact that they were not paid when inclement weather prevented them from working. The Pleasantville Corporation quickly agreed to pay for the rainy days, but the rate-of-pay issue lingered.

In approving the Project's terms the Bahamas government had, in fact, agreed to use the existing labour rates for the employment of local workers; these rates had been established in 1936 and did not take into account inflation as a result of the war. The current unskilled-worker rate was four shillings for an eight-hour working day, and for some reason this same rate was applied to semi-skilled workers. This meant that the Bahamian unskilled worker was making one-third of his American counterpart, and the semi-skilled worker was making about one-tenth of what the American at the same skill level was making. It was no small task for these workers to clear the pine forest and then to carry out the arduous tasks of establishing runways and associated buildings required for an airport.

While there were not many American workers on the job, the large force of Bahamian workers was nevertheless dissatisfied with the vast discrepancies in pay. The pay issue became a rallying cry for the workers who chanted "We want more money!" and formed a labour union. The workers asserted that it was impossible for them to live on four shillings a day.

Regardless of the disquiet that eventually erupted into a riot, both airports were eventually completed. What was originally known as Satellite Field was developed into the main airport, which later became the successful and attractive international airport and welcome centre to what is today a highly profitable tourist economy in The Bahamas. Oakes Field was developed as a modern sports centre now named for one of our late sports icons, the track and field athlete Thomas A. Robinson.

THE RIOT

Workers' disatisfaction was taken to the next stage on Tuesday, May 26, 1942, when the executive committee of the Bahamas Federation of Labour, led by its president, Charles Rhodriguez, asked the government labour officer for additional wages for labourers employed on the two projects at Satellite Field and the main Oakes Field airports. The workers had been looking forward to higher wages that they fully expected to receive from their foreign employers, and felt aggrieved that American labourers were being paid more than Bahamians for the same jobs.

With neither management nor the government making any meaningful effort to resolve the wage dispute, the grumbling among the labourers, particularly the younger ones, escalated on the morning of Monday, June 1, 1942, to the point where more than a thousand workers who had gathered at the work site refused to clock in, shouting, "No work today!"

Fed up with continuing their unanswered pleas for higher wages and improved conditions, the labourers lay down their tools and on a prearranged signal angrily strode from the construction site of the military airfield being built in the southwestern section of the island. Marching with homemade clubs made from the limbs of trees in the pine forest in which the airfield was being developed, they made their way along the nearby "interfield" road, which had been developed by the airfield workers to access the new air base and paralleled the coastal road into town. It was on this new road that they continued their trek past the Oakes Airport, the site of the second military airfield then under construction. The road took on the name "Burma Road" after the recent retreat by the British from the Japanese along the main supply route to Burma from China—the Burma Road. At this point, hundreds more workers from that work site joined in the march, making the group twice as large and doubly boisterous. The presence of police as the crowd grew made the situation worse, as the volatile group marched from Oakes Field toward downtown Nassau, looking for someone in authority to whom they could address their concerns. They turned north onto Nassau Street loudly screaming what had become a stentorian battle cry.

"Burma Road declare war on de Conchy-Joe" was being repeated in rhythmic unison by a throng of angry souls. "Conchy-Joe" was a slang term applied to any Bahamian of Caucasian descent whose family had been in The Bahamas for a long time. The native white Bahamians are generally proud to be Conchy-Joes, and consider the term endearing rather than racially insensitive. When the local protesters were "declaring war on de Conchy-Joe" they were, however, railing not only against their local white employers but also the white Bahamians who controlled the economic and political power in The Bahamas at that time. As a rallying chant, this defiant theme was occasionally alternated with familiar patriotic songs, such as "We'll Never Let the Old Flag Fall," sung in a provincial manner as a native version of the patriotic song, "Rule Britannia."

As the workers marched through the main thoroughfares of the crowded over-the-hill communities of Grant's Town and Bain Town, many of the unemployed men standing on the sidewalks along the way joined in the procession, which moved quickly towards the heart of the city. They reached the top of Grant's Town hill on Baillou Hill Road, alongside Western Senior School (now C. R. Walker Senior High School), passed the governor's imposing residence at the top of the hill, stormed down George Street leading downhill past the cathedral, and onward to Bay Street and the heart of the downtown business district. The rowdy group then continued eastward along the middle of Bay Street until they reached Rawson Square, the city centre which housed the Parliament buildings and the official buildings containing the offices of the colonial secretary and other government executives.

Upon arriving at Rawson Square, the crowd had grown to about 1,500 strong as, pushing and shoving, they gathered outside the colonial secretary's office at the corner of Bay Street and Bank Lane, to the east of the Parliament buildings, shouting various demands for increased wages.

At this time, the Duke of Windsor was attending a meeting in Washington, and Leslie Heape was the acting governor.

Many of the protesting workers had gathered outside the colonial secretary's office hoping to speak to Heape, but instead they were addressed by Eric Hallinan, the attorney general. Hallinan's comments further incensed the workers; they saw his remarks as a stalling tactic and, worse, as a threat. When he told them that it had only been through the Duke of Windsor's intervention that they had work, insinuating that they should not only be grateful to have a job but also risked losing their employment if they did not return to work, the enraged crowd responded by breaking windows and looting stores along downtown Bay Street, and within hours had wreaked havoc across a large area of the city buildings of Nassau.

Acting Governor Heape had called some of the labour representatives to Government House while the ruckus was going on downtown, and they were able to persuade some of the crowd to return over the hill to the Southern Recreation Grounds. When the police, led by Commissioner Colonel Reginald Alexander Erskine-Lindop joined them there, the crowd threw rocks and bottles at the officials. In order to disperse the workers and in an attempt to quell further unlawful behavior, the commissioner, accompanied by a group of his officers, took a position outside the Cotton Tree Inn on Blue Hill Road and read aloud the Riot Act. This is the term given to the process of his formally reading the section of the Penal Code in the statute laws of The Bahamas, which provides that a magistrate or other authorized person "shall openly and with a loud voice" make a proclamation in the words of the section of the law which commands all assembled persons to disperse immediately "and peaceably depart to their habitations, or to their lawful business." This section of the law further provides that if twelve or more persons continue to remain riotously assembled, then any peace officer may do anything necessary to disperse the persons assembled or to apprehend them—and those were indeed the dire measures that were taken by the commissioner of police.

Although the rioters had begun to destroy property and tensions were escalating, they were only armed with cutlasses, sticks, and bottles. Nevertheless the police fired gunshots into the crowd. As a result one worker, Roy Johnson, was killed instantly and six others seriously wounded. While it was never officially determined who fired the shots that killed the worker, it was believed to be one of the police officers who attempted to disperse the riotous crowd.

As word of Johnson's killing spread, a large, angry crowd attacked the Southern Police Station, burning the fire engine and ambulance before they continued on to damage the post office and library. The police remobilized and established a military ring around Grant's Town, then declared a curfew. The nighttime quiet, however, did not last long: as soon as the curfew ended at 6:00 a.m. on Tuesday, June 2, hundreds of workers went back downtown, vandalizing more business establishments.

The Duke of Windsor arrived back in Nassau that evening and promptly extended the curfew. The following morning he met with several black leaders, who urged him to act quickly and to publicly rebuke oppression, inequality, and poverty.

The Duke made a national broadcast on the Wednesday evening following the riot, urging calm and a return to work so that negotiations could proceed. The workers did so the following morning and the Duke immediately negotiated a raise of a shilling a day as the minimum wage, with a free midday meal, and an understanding that those engaged in specialized work would be paid above the minimum rate. The curfew was lifted on June 8, in a nationally broadcast address outlining the concessions made.

The Duke established a commission of inquiry to review the causes and effects of the riots. He chose Sir Alison Russell, a non-resident Englishman, along with two white Bahamian merchants. Called the Russell Commission, their report recognized that there were deeper causes for the riots other than the wage dispute, such as economic depression, political inequalities, and deficiencies in social and labour legislation.

The findings of this investigation led to many important and wide-ranging social and political reforms, including a reduction of the life of Parliament from seven to five years; the introduction of a "one man, one ballot" vote; and a rise in taxes to make the wealthy contribute more to the cost of running the country.

The Duke of Windsor, to his credit in at least this instance, did indeed have a calming effect on the events resulting from the riot, and he also put in motion efforts to level the playing field politically between white and black Bahamians.

HIS COMING

D r. C. R. Walker was not a typical black Bahamian of the 1940s. The total population was then just under 70,000, in contrast to the present-day population of over 300,000 residents, which over the course of each year is buttressed with the arrival of more than four million tourists. In 1942 eighty-five percent of the residents were black, as is still the case. Although a relatively high percentage of the present-day Bahamian black community now complete their local education at high school level, with thousands of them each year seeking higher education either at the College of The Bahamas or at many other college campuses abroad, at that time the total number of high school graduates among the entire black community numbered less than five hundred. And barely a dozen or so of these had the means or the opportunity to go on to university. Indeed, the Bahamians who possessed a university degree could be counted on one hand.

Claudius Roland Walker was one of the rare few of his day who had that privilege, pursuing high school and college abroad.

Born in Nassau in 1897 to hard-working parents of humble origin, his father was Claudius F. Walker, a schoolteacher who taught in many of the Family Islands of The Bahamas. His mother, Patience Walker (née Robinson), was a seamstress. As an only child, he was unusually fortunate to have had opportunities beyond those of his peers who were similarly raised, resided, and educated in Grant's Town. At the age of nineteen, he was given the chance to travel to New York City to stay with an uncle who lived there while he studied at Rhodes High School. After completion of his secondary schooling, he entered Howard University in Washington, D.C., followed by medical studies at Meharry Medical College in Nashville, Tennessee, where he graduated as president of his class in 1929. The following year, at the age of thirty-three, he returned home to Nassau as a qualified medical doctor, and entered into private practice with his patient base predominantly in the Grant's Town area of the Southern District, whose residents he also served as elected representative in the House of Assembly for more than twenty years. This impoverished urban area of Nassau encompassed the historic quarters to the rear of Government House where Nassau's black working and servant classes lived.

Dr. Walker had a brilliant mind, a passion for uplifting his people, and a flair for oratory, which captivated the attention of his audience whenever he spoke. An accomplished musician and linguist, he was proficient in Spanish, French, and German, and gifted in mathematics. He was a passionate advocate of educational opportunity for all, and today the oldest public school in the Southern District has been renamed in his honor as the C. R. Walker Senior High School.

Dr. Walker was truly one of his country's most famous native sons, hailing from out of the bosom of the masses, and by his exemplary life and achievements, he depicted a truly positive response to another age-old biblical question: "Can any good thing come out of Nazareth?"

No wonder then that Doc, as he was affectionately called, was a popular, almost hero-worshipped, leader of his fellow black Bahamians, particularly those who lived "over the hill." Here certainly was a champion and spokesperson for the discontented and oppressed labourers, who had vented their desperate feelings of hopelessness and despair in the riotous acts of lawlessness and violence on Bay Street.

As a member of Parliament the good doctor had requested and been granted an urgent audience for himself, together with a delegation of three members of the Bahamas Federation of Labour, to meet with the governor and his Executive Council. Today, such an important delegation would be received in the formal drawing room of the governor's mansion; but these men were black, and in 1942 black men had never been received inside Government House. So this meeting took place in the upper-floor ballroom of the annex building, the ground floor of which also housed the offices of the governor and his staff.

The atmosphere was tense.

Acting as spokesman for the group, Dr. Walker arose from his seat and stood respectfully but unflinchingly before the former king of England. Two years had passed since the Duke of Windsor's arrival, yet critical questions about the Duke's character and leadership remained strong in the minds and hearts of Bahamians. Was he the one who would lead The Bahamas to greatness—indeed, was it "He that cometh?" Who, indeed, was this royal person? The future of The Bahamas depended on the answers.

In a clear, forthright, but quiet voice, Dr. Walker began his oration by citing the workers' grievances and eloquently pleading their cause.

"Your Royal Highness, Gentlemen:

"The underlying causes for this social unrest are manifold. We are in the majority but we have minority problems. We are poorly housed, poorly fed and poorly educated. Truth to tell, we are the wretched of the earth.

"Many years ago, England and American missionaries walked among us intent on souls to save and bodies to enslave, until one day one of my ancestral brothers was forced to remark, 'Fadder, when firs' you come to Bahamas, you had da Bible and we had da land. Today, Fadder, we gat da Bible and you gat da land."[36]

With that biting remark, Dr. Walker was giving vent to the deep resentment which many Bahamians still hold against white land-owners who, then as now, controlled most of the expensive beach frontage and valuable acreage, which formerly was almost entirely in the hands of their forefathers as freed slaves.

The previous hundred years had given rise to a complete reversal in land ownership. Most of the white missionaries and merchants, in the process of proselytizing and educating the land-rich but money-poor former slaves and their descendants, were reputed to have exercised undue influence on the unlettered and unsuspecting native inhabitants in order to seize their land. They ended up as the landed gentry while the black population found itself confined and huddled in small, poor communities over the hill and on the outskirts, such as the villages of Fox Hill, Carmi-chael, and Gambier.

After a brief pause, intended to allow his listeners to hear and digest the full force and effect of the point he had just made, the

36 R. Fawkes, *The Faith that Moved the Mountain,* Nassau, Nassau Guardian, 1979, p. 28.

doctor eloquently summarized the underlying inequities of land ownership:

> "Land is an important factor in the production of wealth. When strangers grab the land of the natives they are tampering not only with their economic existence but with their cultural and political lives as well. That is why 'land snatching' as it is practised today is the most concrete proof of the thorough enslavement of a people to an alien will."[37]

Walker then showed the concrete effects of outside land ownership on the electoral process, and outlined abuses in the system in which Bahamians effectively had little or no say in the way they were governed.

> "For over two hundred years, a locally based Governor vested with autocratic powers directed the affairs of The Bahamas on behalf of the British Crown. He did this through a wholly appointed Executive Council, a wholly appointed Legislative Council, and a House of Assembly, the members of which were elected once every seven years on a male franchise hemmed in by property qualifications, company and plural voting. All males were required to vote openly, and face victimization if their choice of candidates displeased their employers. More than half of the adult population—the women—could not vote at all."[38]

Moreover, the wealthy were allowed to travel among the islands where they held property or owned businesses and cast

37 Fawkes, p. 28.

38 Ibid., p. 29.

multiple votes in each of these locations over a three-week period.

> "This iniquitous electoral system continues to secure the political and economic supremacy of the white landed gentry. They own and manage both land and labor through numerous attorneys, accountants, foremen and skilled artisans."[39]

This was much more than a powerfully worded accusation. Indeed, it was a cogent condemnation of an existing electoral system which perpetuated in power a white merchantocracy whose racial makeup represented a mere fifteen percent of the population. The "coloureds," as the black population was termed in the vernacular of the 1940s, were mostly poorly educated and scarcely propertied.

It could not be successfully argued that Dr. Walker was employing histrionics in order to advance the case of an ambitious but frustrated leader of the black community. This is borne out by the fact that both past governors of The Bahamas, the Duke's immediate predecessors, had each independently sent earlier confidential reports to the secretary of state in England which provided irrefutable corroboration of Dr. Walker's assertions.

Shortly before completing his term as governor, Sir Bede Clifford sent a report dated April 12, 1937, to William Ormsby-Gore, the secretary of state for the colonies, in which he mentioned his misgiving over the rapid increase of property ownership by U.S. citizens residing in The Bahamas, thereby giving them the potential for controlling the government. Sir Bede explained that "elections to the House of Assembly are today decided in favour of the candidate who puts up the most money, and the amount seldom exceeds a couple of hundred pounds. While aliens themselves

---

39 Fawkes, p. 29.

cannot become Members, they could exercise considerable influence by the expenditure of a negligible sum."[40]

Sir Bede Clifford was succeeded in office by the former colonial secretary of Bermuda, Charles Dundas, who was knighted the following year on being appointed governor of The Bahama Islands. Although Governor Dundas was fully briefed on the political landscape of the colony before he arrived, he soon experienced firsthand how elections were run. He had been in office but a few months when a specially called election, known as a by-election, was held in June 1938 in the Western District to fill the seat in the House of Assembly left vacant by the Honorable A. F. Adderley, who had the month before been elevated to membership in the Legislative Council.

A world-famous resident, Harry Oakes, who had moved to The Bahamas from Canada only four years earlier and was reputed to be one of the wealthiest men in the British Empire, obtained ninety percent of the vote for this vacant seat despite the fact that he remained in England throughout the period of the election and the brief period of its preceding campaign, which was managed for him by an agent.

His worthy opponent was Milo Butler, a popular black Bahamian merchant who operated two grocery shops and also held a franchise for the daily delivery of ice to homes mostly in Nassau's urban black community, in those days before household refrigerators were commonplace or even affordable. This candidate, who hailed from the small out-island of Rum Cay, was an outspoken champion who publicly railed against the racial ills and prejudices which were then the order of the day. He barely obtained ten percent of the vote and lost his deposit of fifty pounds. Thirty-five

---

40 Sir B. Clifford, Ormsby-Gore, W., *Colonial Office Papers CO23/594/8,* Bahamas Department of Archives, 12 April 1937.

years later Butler was to become the first Bahamian governor general of an independent Bahamas, after a vibrant political career as a member of Parliament from 1939 until 1973, both as an opposition member and later as a minister of government. In this latter year he resigned his seat to take office as governor general and received the accolade of knighthood from Queen Elizabeth with an award of Knight Grand Cross of the Most Distinguished Order of St. Michael and St. George (GCMG).

In his report on the 1938 by-election, Governor Dundas referred to details of the shameful campaign tactics employed by Oakes's agents, and cited this corrupt practice as a compelling reason to bolster his resolve to introduce legislation for a secret ballot. He stressed the point that "prior to the election I had heard that votes could be bought."[41]

Interestingly, Oakes sat as a member of the House for only a year, being elevated to the Legislative Council in 1939. His election in 1938 was the last occasion that the system of open voting was used, and the last time the right to vote was confined to male British citizens over twenty-one years of age, born or resident in The Bahamas, who owned or had actual possession of land of a value not less than £300 sterling. Paradoxically, while this excluded all women and a majority of Bahamian men, a company incorporated and registered in The Bahamas had the right to vote through one of its directors, provided it owned or was in possession of land of the requisite value. To make matters worse, a male individual or a company could register as a voter, and actually vote during the same election in as many electoral constituencies as land was owned.

41 Sir B. Clifford, Ormsby-Gore, W., *Colonial Office Papers CO23/594/8,* Bahamas Department of Archives, 12 April 1937.

Secret-ballot voting had been authorized by law in July 1939, but was limited to New Providence and for a trial period only. Accordingly, by the time the Duke arrived in August 1940, only a limited exercise of the system was in effect.

At the time that Dr. Walker was making his impassioned presentation to his governor, the secret ballot had already been tested in the by-election in 1939, and again for the constituencies in New Providence in the general elections of 1942. Although these reforms removed some of the corrupt practices of the electoral process, the franchise was still withheld from most Bahamians; the law had not been extended to the whole colony, and women were not allowed to vote until three elections later when the general elections of 1962 were held.

It is therefore not surprising that at the time of Dr. Walker's speech, he focused on the continuing unequal social order and justice system of the day, as he continued in that vein:

"Next on the social pyramid were the merchants. The high prices of the middle class group played havoc with the poor on whose shoulders fell the full burden of an administrative system in which the rich pay no income taxes whatsoever."[42]

Dr. Walker then made reference to an onerous peculiarity in the justice system, long since abolished, which allowed a litigant in certain types of civil cases, or even in certain criminal cases regarded as involving highly technical or difficult features, to apply for a special jury to be empaneled from a list of individuals who met particular qualifications and were thought to be better educated than ordinary jurors. The loophole was often used

42 Fawkes, p. 29.

to populate juries that would likely punish those who spoke out against existing unfair practices.

> "Warrants for the arrest of ringleaders—would-be social reformers—are frequently issued for the most trivial of offences. In this way the law is made a weapon to club the natives into submission. Since there is no Bahamian Court of Appeal from a conviction on an indictable offence, the English judges with the help of their 'special' white juries often mete out draconian sentences against the black people.
>
> "Recently, my brother told me the other day, that when Columbus made his historic voyage to the New World the English simultaneously dispatched two ships from London. The name of the first ship was Law, and of the second, Justice.
>
> "The ship, Law, arrived safely into port, but, Gentlemen, Justice was lost somewhere in the mid-Atlantic."[43]

Being the skillful orator that he was, Dr. Walker now saw that the royal listener and his entourage were paying self-conscious yet rapt attention. The former king leaned forward as he hung on every word of the speaker, a short rotund figure with a receding hairline, whose eyes sparkled almost mischievously as he spoke. At this point, Walker expanded the scope of his discourse to expose the racist practices of the day within a broad historical perspective.

> "But something equally as precious as Justice was also lost, and this was the real tragedy. Untold millions, uprooted from their native cultures in Africa, were scattered as slaves in North, Central, and South America, in the Caribbean, and elsewhere. Diaspora, which

43 Fawkes, p. 29.

means a scattering or dispersal of a people, originally referred to the Jewish historical experience; but it has never been more descriptive than when applied to the children of Africa.

"We Bahamians are the sons and grandsons, the daughters and grand daughters, of those who arrived. We seek today to reclaim that which was snatched from us over 300 years ago—our dignity and self-respect as human beings.

"During the interval between then and now, we have become the most brain-washed people of the world. We were made to believe that we were not fit to govern ourselves. You see, teachers and missionaries did not tell us that there was a period in ancient history—at a time when Rome was barbarous, and Greece slept—when Africa flourished with its own governments, economic systems, military forces, religious and social organizations. Indeed, in the very beginning of mankind, the African nation of Egypt occupied a central role in world history.

"We were taught that our ancestors contributed nothing to the advancement of civilization. Yet it was common knowledge that Africans were the first to practise agriculture—the first of the cultures—along the banks of the Niger River. Africa was the place where mankind first fashioned tools—a significant step in the evolution of civilization. Neither did they tell my people, Gentlemen, that the earliest known pottery was created in Africa more than thirty thousand years ago, during the Paleolithic period of the Stone Age."[44]

Dr. Walker, as he had done throughout his presentation, then took what could be perceived as an academic discussion and showed how it affected the daily lives of black Bahamians:

44 Fawkes, pp. 29–30.

WHAT MANNER OF MAN IS THIS?

WHAT MANNER OF MAN IS THIS?

WHAT MANNER OF MAN IS THIS?

"It is a tragic fact that Bahamians have suffered many a serious social and psychological trauma from the decades of contempt and calumny which characterized traditional Western historical thought on the subject of Africa. Most of our fathers and mothers were compelled to live out their lives in submission to the dominant cultural values and attitudes of the hostile whites. They were forced to tolerate the racist ideologies of their white countrymen in order to survive. It is a psychological truism that an oppressed and rejected people soon come to see themselves through the eyes of their oppressors. As a result, the black man soon learned how to hate himself and others of his own race.

"In the past, the schoolroom was not primarily an educational institution but a political one which sought only to maintain the power base of the white colonialist society."[45]

At that point, Dr. Walker sensed that the interest of the Duke and his Council members had been fully awakened. The Duke, in particular, was reacting in the manner of a juror who had been completely entranced by the cogent arguments, which seemed at times alternately those of a prosecutor and defence counsel. It was now time to confront the pressing issue at hand: the wage dispute which had provoked the rioters needed to be resolved with an increase in the workers' favour. In his most forceful tone, the doctor began an impassioned condemnation of the labour practices of the day:

"The Emancipation Act of the United Kingdom Parliament, though designed to come into force in the Colonies on August 1, 1834, did not immediately give the slave his freedom. There was a compulsory 'apprenticeship' period similar in all but name to indentured labour. Now over one hundred years after the Emancipation Act, the

45 Fawkes, pp. 30–31.

colonial bosses offer sons of former slaves four shillings per day! O ye nominal Christians! Might not the son of an African slave ask you: 'Learned you this from your own god?' Is not the labourer worthy of his hire? What dignity is there in slaving for a dollar a day?

"Can a man maintain his self-respect when he cannot feed himself and his family? I think not.

"Can a dollar a day pay his medical expenses if he falls ill on the job site? I think not.

"Can the poor purchase enough food to strengthen him [sic] to perform heavy duty labour efficiently? No, Gentlemen. No!"[46]

Once again, using the power of his oratory, Dr. Walker outlined how the inequality of the wages, on a practical level, affected the people of his country—not only the Bahamian workers but the wealthier classes in the audience as well:

"Poor wages mean a poor community, and a poor community is the breeding ground for crime and disease. Furthermore, if these labourers are not paid a decent wage they will not have the purchasing power to buy the goods in the Bay Street stores.

"Gentlemen, your own self-interest should persuade you to give my brothers a decent wage!

"Will the labourers return to their job site for four shillings per day?

"Why should men who worked for four shillings yesterday want eight shillings today?"[47]

Again, Doc sought to drive home his plea, the main point of his entire speech, with another anecdote; but this time he used an allegorical homespun tale:

46 Fawkes, pp. 31–32.

47 Ibid. p. 32.

"Pray, let me tell you a story.

"My eldest son's bitch had a litter of pups. One day a neighbor came and asked the price for one.

"My son replied, 'One shilling for each puppy.'

"The following day, the same lady returned with the shilling to complete the purchase. On approaching Roland she was rebuffed.

"'No, no,' he said, 'the puppies are now two shillings each!'

"'Yesterday, puppy one shilling; today, puppy, two shillings! How come?' she inquired.

"'Well you see, Ma'am, yesterday the puppies' eyes were closed; today, their eyes are opened. Yesterday, they were blind; today, they can see.'

"Gentlemen, the scales have been peeled off the eyes of the labourers. They now see opportunities beyond their status quo. They have discovered new insights—new strength in unity—and no one can purchase their labour now for so cheap a price as four shillings a day. The winds of change of World War II have blown in their direction and they have inhaled the air of freedom. Once they have tasted it, they can no longer live without it."[48]

However riveting he perceived his speech to have been, Walker was not content to merely speak to the audience as a group. Instead, with a gallery of attentive and powerful witnesses, he ended most dramatically with a personal coup de grâce directed pointedly at the man he wanted most to affect with the power of his words and the urgency of his message:

"And now I wish to conclude with a personal word to His Royal Highness, the Duke of Windsor himself.

48 Fawkes, p. 32.

"Two years ago when the radio waves brought the news of Your Royal Highness' appointment as Governor of The Bahamas, the Deaf heard, and the Dumb spoke, the Blind saw and the Crippled leaped for joy. Your reputation as an humanitarian and King had preceded you.

"'Surely', we said to ourselves, 'the Duke of Windsor will not allow us to continue to live amidst social inequities that sap our self-respect and prevent us from attaining our full status as first-class citizens.'

"Fifty-four Governors have preceded Your Excellency, but not one ever brought a ray of hope to the poor and oppressed.

"We believe that you are not just another Governor for one class of people, but the Governor for all colours and classes of people.

"In faith believing, I ask on behalf of all my brothers and sisters, 'Art thou he that cometh or look we for another?'"[49]

With this time-honoured question—first put to Jesus by John the Baptist in Matthew 11:13—Dr. Walker dramatically ended one of the most famous speeches in Bahamian political history.

A pregnant silence and palpable tension fell upon the room. Dr. Walker was satisfied that his performance had made a strong impression on his royal listener. Without saying more, he made a respectful bow and withdrew to his seat.

Although the Duke then smilingly thanked Dr. Walker for his presentation, a sombre mood nevertheless remained as many high expectations were riding on Dr. Walker's appeal. Although other Bahamian political leaders had on several previous occasions addressed the world-famous commander in chief in his role as governor in the two years since his arrival, the recent tragic and explosive events of the riot made Dr. Walker's remarks much more dramatic and significant.

49 Fawkes, pp. 32–33.

Dr. Walker's brilliant oration was, without question, the most stirring address to be made to the royal governor during the entire five-year term of his office. Although the Duke was accustomed to hearing the fine oratory of some of the greatest masters of the English language of his day—such as Winston Churchill, Stanley Baldwin, Neville Chamberlain, and Dr. Cosmo Gordon Laing, the Archbishop of Canterbury, as well as actors in the noblest theatrical performances of that period—he was visibly moved.

After Dr. Walker took his seat, the governor explained that the scale of wages, about which the rioting Bahamian workmen were complaining, had not been negotiated locally, but had in fact been settled between the American and British governments when the contract to build the bases was negotiated. However, the Duke assured the doctor and his delegation that he would again take up the matter of wages with officials in Washington, and revert in short order to advise them of his results.

The impassioned presentation, from someone who knew at first hand the impoverishment and substandard quality of life of many of his fellow Bahamians, had challenged the imported official of royal blood and high station to deal with the major concerns which continued to beset the people whom he had been appointed to govern. These issues included the disproportionate systems relating to suffrage, land ownership, job opportunities and fair wages, the poor quality (and general unavailability) of higher education, racial inequality, and the unfair social order. These were all struggles that went to the very core needs of all Bahamians.

Although Walker's incisive question, which reflected those very inequities and hopes, was unequivocally directed to His Royal Highness, it had yet to be answered by action:

"Art thou he that cometh, or look we for another?"

THE BAY STREET FIRE

Prior to September 2004, when devastating Hurricane Francis caused widespread devastation throughout the Bahamian islands, June 1942 was chronicled as the most tragic month in the entire history of The Bahamas.

At the beginning of that month the Burma Road Riot had erupted in full force, leaving death and extensive damage in its wake. Just twenty-seven days later, on Sunday, June 28, the residents of Nassau were traumatized by an early-morning fire alarm, which heralded the terrifying news of "Bay Street burnin' down!" Businesses housed in the heart of the city center, which over the years had become well-known landmarks in this oldest section of Nassau, were rapidly being destroyed. The flames raged furiously and unabated early Sunday morning between one and six o'clock, moving along the western end of central Bay Street, on its southern side, and up both sides of George Street to King Street.

Sadly, in no part of the city were the buildings more closely clustered together than in this oldest section of Nassau Town. As the

Monday edition of the *Nassau Guardian* reported the following after-noon, from the moment the alarm sounded at 1:18 a.m. on Sunday, the situation was considered most grave. The flames first burst out from the back of Rogers Juvenile Shop, owned by Glen Raymond Rogers, and quickly caught the roof of the adjoining Black's Candy Kitchen. Both these businesses were located just to the west of Market Street and on the south side of Bay Street. Fanned by a fairly strong northeasterly breeze, the fires spread from one building to another until the entire western end of the block became a raging inferno. When it was seen that the fire was spreading along this southern side of Bay Street to George Street, the fire engines proceeded immediately to the harbour front by way of an alley running northwards off Bay Street, between the Ice House and the Public Market in order to access water from the harbour for their hoses.

According to the account in the *Nassau Daily Tribune*, before day-break fourteen buildings and nearly thirty businesses were destroyed. The loss was estimated at approximately a half-million pounds sterling.

Citizens of every rank and hue hurried from their homes as news of the calamity spread as quickly as the fire itself. They fear-lessly joined the growing ranks of volunteers who courageously, and with little concern for their personal risk, rendered bodily assistance to residents who were forced to leave their blazing or smoke-filled homes. Others joined one of the several relay lines helping to save valuable goods being salvaged from the burning buildings. Considerable quantities of items, some badly damaged by water, were retrieved by the untiring efforts of hundreds of first-time firefighters, including the royal governor and his Duchess.

They had arrived on the scene just ten minutes after the first fire engine appeared, coming down the hill from the their imposing official mansion at the top of George Street to join the many volunteers who assisted the fire brigades in manning the water hoses. The Duke, blackened with soot and drenched to the skin, personally directed volunteer groups working tirelessly from 1:30 a.m. until dawn.

The Duchess of Windsor, who was president of The Bahamas Branch of the British Red Cross, together with other Red Cross personnel and many unsolicited assistants who had joined them from the crowd of anxious onlookers, were inside the Red Cross centre feverishly packing and securing what they could of the threatened supplies for removal to safer quarters.

The centre was housed in the locally famous Brick Store building, an impressive landmark at the junction of George and Marlborough Streets. It was originally built in 1901 by T. H. C. Lofthouse of Bahamian songwriting fame, but at the time of the fire it was owned by Sir Harry Oakes, who had permitted the Red Cross to use it as its main centre since the outbreak of World War II. This red-brick building was erected on a vacant lot previously owned by the British War Office; it adjoined, to the east, the old officers quarters, which had been the site of the resident British garrison in earlier colonial times at a location now occupied by the British Colonial Hilton Hotel.

It was in an effort to save this building and the Red Cross supplies within, that the Duke and two of his aides-de-camp could be seen manning one of the fire hoses and helping to direct the water stream as flames threatened to engulf the structure. It was, nevertheless, completely demolished.

Indeed, George Street, which like Bay Street was one of the original and well-known thoroughfares of Old Nassau, lost all of its landmark buildings on both sides north of the Christ Church Cathedral, which was just a stone's throw from the Red Cross centre. An imposing historic structure, the cathedral was the fifth in its line to stand on the same site as the first church erected in

New Providence soon after 1670, before the settlement of Charles Town came to be known as the town of Nassau.

After the fire had raged for several hours, smoke was suddenly spotted on the roof of the cathedral and it was feared that this century-old church would also soon succumb to the flames. Without warning, however, and as if by a miracle, a shower of rain suddenly came down and soaked the smoking roof, simultaneously energizing the gallant efforts of the firefighters and volunteers and saving the historic and beloved house of worship.

As a result of lengthy investigations, Glen Rogers, the shopkeeper of the fabric store where the fire had started, was charged with arson and intent to defraud an insurance company. The case opened in the Supreme Court of The Bahamas on August 12, 1942, before Chief Justice Sir Oscar Daly. Arrested a month earlier, Rogers had been denied bail, and was remanded in custody pending his trial. After a two-week trial, he was convicted on August 26 by a jury verdict of ten to two, and sentenced to jail for four years.

The tragic Bay Street Fire, like the riot, led to a more favourable public impression of the Duke of Windsor. Many admired (and fondly remember) how the Duke stood side by side with hundreds of firefighting volunteers, fire hose in hand, covered with soot and water. On that day, he was seen as a regular citizen willing to do his part. In fact, this was another example of the Duke's acting as a decisive leader: directing the many volunteers and rising to the occasion in the case of an emergency. Later, he could be seen on several occasions walking along Bay Street and inspecting the fire-damaged buildings. His interest provided a great inspiration to the owners to carry out the necessary restoration to their properties and their businesses. The rebuilding took place soon after, and the western end of Bay Street was restored to its former character.

THE CONTRACT

1943–1965

In September 1942, just three months after the violent riot and the devastating Bay Street Fire, and while the world was still in the midst of World War II, the Duchess of Windsor wrote to her Aunt Bessie saying, "The Negroes here are busy complaining, now that the base is nearing completion and some of them are being laid off."[50]

Her observations were indeed correct: unemployment was growing as a result of the recent completion of the two airfields constructed in western New Providence. This was quickly becoming a potentially devastating economic situation for The Bahamas and thus of great concern to local government members.

To address this potentially explosive situation, reminiscent of the employment conditions that caused the Burma Road Riot of 1942, the Duke negotiated an agreement with Washington for the recruitment of up to 5,000 Bahamian workers to be employed as

50 Bloch, p. 281.

agricultural labourers in the United States. In what was one of the most outstanding achievements of his governorship, this program was seen as an extension of the project to build the local airfields; although some continued to call it by that same name, this foreign employment arrangement was afterwards generally referred to as the Contract, which referred to the document the workers were required to sign.

The agreement was mutually beneficial to both The Bahamas and the United States in that Bahamians needed jobs and the United States needed labourers. Through this program the developing unemployment situation in The Bahamas was reversed; and in the United States, labourers were now available to fill the shortage of workers, which the country was experiencing because most of their able-bodied workers either enlisted or were conscripted to join the war effort, thus vacating essential jobs in the agricultural and industrial areas.

The Contract stipulated that workers had to be at least eighteen years of age, medically fit, employed solely in agriculture, and not drafted into military service. Each worker signed a personal contract and the term was either for six or nine months. A portion of the wages paid, normally 25 percent, was withheld to be paid to the workers' family in The Bahamas or otherwise deposited in the Post Office Savings Bank in the name of the worker. This ensured that the worker took care of his responsibilities back home, or would have some funds saved upon his return from the States.

The *Nassau Daily Tribune* and the *Nassau Guardian*, in their respective publications on Saturday, March 20, 1943, published an official statement by the government about the arrangement. The official statement, which followed a visit by labour officers from Washington, D.C., read:

1. The Department of Agriculture of the United States and the Bahamas Government signed an agreement on the 16th of March providing for the importation of Bahamian workers into the United States for Agricultural employment in Florida and the adjoining states. This was announced today by the Secretary of Agriculture Claude R. Wickard.

2. The agreement is the second to be negotiated by the United States Government for the introduction of foreign workers to assist with the nation's war-time food production in areas where there is a labour shortage.

3. The general conditions pertaining to employment of Bahamian workers are the same as those which apply to other seasonal farm workers recruited by the United States Government.

4. The agreement provides for a contract to be entered into between the individual worker and the Department of Agriculture of the United States and provides for a guaranteed minimum rate of pay and for a subsistence allowance for a certain proportion of the period when the worker might be unemployed; the worker generally shall be entitled to such benefits as obtained for all farm workers in the United States.

5. It should be clearly understood that recruitment will be purely voluntary but that any worker who signs the contract with the American Department of Agriculture will be required to remit, in the case of a married man, to a family allowance fund and in the case of a single man, to a savings fund, a fixed sum. These remittances will be collected by the United States Authorities and remitted to the Bahamas Government which will be responsible for disbursement in the Colony.

6. The agreement between the American and the Bahamas Governments has been concluded in order to provide the necessary machinery for the prompt and smooth movement of workers

when the United States Department of Agriculture decides that such importation of Bahamian labour is necessary.

7. Arrangements have been made for the recruitment and necessary medical examination to take place at the various Out Island settlements as well as in New Providence. The recruitment and examination will be undertaken by United States officials in conjunction with a representative of the Bahamas Government.

8. The signatories to the agreement are Mr. Fred Marrell, Assistant Director of Agriculture, Labour Administration, and the Colonial Secretary on behalf of the Bahamas Government.[51]

The details of the Contract were read into the records of the Bahamian Parliament at its meeting on March 31, 1943, as Message No. 52 from the governor. This was followed by a special radio broadcast by the governor on Sunday, April 4, 1943, who said: "I wanted to talk to you for a few minutes this morning about the forthcoming recruitment of Bahamian workers for agricultural labour in Florida."

The governor said that while details under the agreement were made public in the press, "There always seem to be a certain number of people who fail to grasp all the essential details so that false and contradictory rumours get into circulation and people get puzzled and fail to appreciate the true facts of the matter in question."[52]

In order to straighten out any doubts, he emphasized and explained a few salient features of the whole scheme.

"The first point I want to make, therefore, is to impress on all desirous of going to Florida, that they are being recruited for

51 Government Notice, "Bahamian Labour for US Farms," *Nassau Daily Tribune,* 20 March 1943.

52 Radio broadcast, Governor, The Duke of Windsor, 4 April, 1943.

agricultural work only or work immediately connected with the agricultural production. It should further be clearly understood that Bahamian workers will not be permitted to move from one job to another except under the auspices of the United States Department of Agriculture with whom they will have entered into a Contract. This also implies that they will continue to work in America for as long as the United States Government requires them.

"The second point I want to clarify is the actual procedure of recruitment of the workers for Florida, which will be carried out by a party of officials from the United States Department of Agriculture, who have already arrived in Nassau for the purpose and who will work in the closest cooperation with the Labour Office and the Staff of the Labour Bureau. . . . I am authorized to announce that the United States Department of Agriculture are following their usual procedure in the recruitment of agricultural labour in that they will not consider any applicants who are engaged in useful or essential employment at the present time."[53]

The governor went on to speak about ensuring that the Out Islands were adequately represented.

"Provision is also being made for the recruitment of 2,000 women but in the whole process of recruitment, I wish it be remembered that the Bahamas Government made a definite promise to Out Islanders, when large numbers began to be laid off from the Project last December, that those who ceased to be employed on New Providence and who returned immediately to their Out Island districts, would be given first consideration in the event of Bahamian labour being required for Florida.

53 Radio broadcast, 4 April, 1943.

"My third point is to explain how The Bahamas have their local manpower problem just the same as America, only in miniature. While 5,000 people are needed immediately in Florida, it is essential that work on the Project continue, employing as it does around 2,000 men for a few more months."[54]

He then spoke of the possibility of a number of permanent job opportunities associated with the Royal Air Force and other civilian postings.

"We must hold a strong reserve of peasant farmers and labourers on the Out Islands to raise stock, vegetables and subsistence crops against the day, may be not far distant, when America will have to cut her exports of foodstuffs to The Bahamas so drastically that we would be faced with a very serious shortage indeed.

"Taking it all in all, I consider the fact that there is a demand for 5,000 of our people in Florida as a distinct advantage to the whole community."[55]

Moreover he reassured Bahamians,

"To all those who are eventually selected to go to Florida by the American recruiting officials, I would like to say this: I am satisfied that the terms of their contract with the United States Government are fair and generous and that the arrangements made for the transportation of the first batches to Miami, although not exactly luxurious, are at any rate, adequate. It must be difficult for most of you to realize the colossal strain on United Nations' shipping at this crucial stage of the war and I can assure you it is to a great extent the

54 Radio broadcast, 4 April, 1943.

55 Ibid.

proximity of the Bahama Islands to the mainland of America that has influenced the United States Government in their choice of this Colony as a convenient source of supply of agricultural workers."[56]

The governor added some cautionary words as well:

"At the same time, I feel that a word of advice to all prospective workers for Florida will not be untimely and is in fact necessary. If would-be applicants have got any idea or notion that this opportunity to work in Florida means a chance to 'see America' as opposed to an Exchange Controlled Confinement within the Colony for the duration, with the option to quit whenever they feel so inclined—then, they had better stay away from the recruiting centres. All who present themselves for acceptance as workers in Florida must be prepared to work and be honest in their intention to work hard and regard the offer of employment in America as a privilege to be contributing to the general war effort. Let there be no mistake about this, for the consequences will be grave for all those who betray the confidence that the signing of the contract with the United States Government places on them."[57]

The Duke continued on a more positive note giving the good character of the Bahamian population his vote of confidence:

"On the other hand, I am sure that the majority who wants to go will have no other motive than to give their best in this enterprise, for besides helping America's food production, they will be gaining unique experience in scientific agricultural methods which will stand them in good stead for all time. They will be going in the

56 Radio broadcast, 4 April, 1943.

57 Ibid.

neighbouring State of Florida where Bahamians are well known and where they will find many relatives.

"And they will be going to a great and friendly Country, which has staked its fortunes with the British in the defence of the things we have been taught to believe in."[58]

The governor promised a continued personal interest to ensure that the United States did indeed fulfill its side of the agreement:

"I will make it my business later on to visit the areas where Bahamian workers will be operating in order that I may see for myself that all is well with them. I wish them all Godspeed and success in America and a safe return on the completion of their undertakings, confident that as Bahamians they will maintain in a foreign land the traditions of the Flag under which they were born."

Recruitment for the Contract began the next day on April 5, 1943, and it was reported that at its peak period in July 1944 a total of 5,762 Bahamians were employed via The Contract, which at that time represented one-twelfth of the entire population.

Representative of so many of these labourers were Frank "Curly" Johnson and Alfred "Buller" Albury from Harbour Island, who were in the first contingent of 1,850 Bahamian men and women to go to the States. They first set out by boat but were turned back because of German submarine patrols, but left again on May 6, 1943, on Pan American Airways from Oakes Field. Both started their employment in Hastings, Florida, in a camp that housed 1,500 labourers living in tents; many were Bahamians, including fourteen men and Retta Albury from Harbour Island. Frank was chosen as a cook because he was the only one able to cook peas and

---

58 Radio broadcast, 4 April, 1943.

rice. There were three kitchens, each with a Bahamian cook who prepared typical meals of 100 pounds of grits and 200 pounds of peas cooked on a wood fire. On a typical day they woke at daylight and ended their work just before dark. They received mail twice a week. While Alfred moved on to Norfolk, Virginia, New York, and Minnesota, Frank went to pick corn in Minnesota, where he earned $21.20 per day. Frank laboured for five years and Alfred for a total of eight years, each gaining valuable experience and much higher earnings than they could have earned at home.[59]

Workers experienced difficult and in some cases even dangerous conditions on some of the farms. One report from a worker in Vero Beach, Florida, records that while he and others were working in Wabasoo, "On the beach side the mosquitoes were there like you never saw in your life, and you could rake your hand and grab a handful of them." This report goes on to say that the mosquitoes were "so bad that they had to smoke the trees with a tractor while they picked the fruit."[60] Other reports contained incidents of encountering poisonous snakes while preparing previously uncultivated fields.[61]

Workers were sometimes employed in several states; for example, harvesting citrus or sugar cane or beans in Florida, tobacco in Tennessee, corn in Minnesota, apples in New York, and peanuts in North Carolina. Some workers were also employed to care for livestock, while others were employed as cooks in the labour camps, or as maintenance workers for farm equipment.

59 A. & J. Lawlor, *The Harbour Island Story,* Oxford, MacMillan Education, 2008, pp. 258–259.

60 S. Miller interviewed by Oral History team, College of The Bahamas, 1991; Thompson, Tracey L. "Remembering the Contract: Recollections of Bahamians," *The International Journal of Bahamian Studies,* accessed from http://journals.sfu.ca/cob/index.php/files/article/view/169/217, 18 June 2012.

61 H. R. Bethel, interviewed by Oral History team, College of The Bahamas, 1992; Ibid.

There were a number of labour camps in which hundreds of workers lived. These included the Okeechobee Farm Labour Supply Center in Belle Glade, Florida, which was well known to Bahamian workers as it accommodated over 800 in the mid-1940s. Some workers also lived on private farms, or in tents, in addition to the barracks normally provided. Married couples were allowed to live by themselves in separate quarters. Although accommodations were generally basic, they did include amenities such as running water and electricity.

The Contract also made particular reference to anti-discriminatory practices by providing that black workers were not to suffer any form of racial discrimination; notwithstanding that provision there were still many reported incidences of racial discrimination, particularly in the southern states.[62]

Although the entire farm labour program had a major impact on The Bahamas, increasing the economic worth of the vast majority of the population, it also had a negative effect on many of the Out Islands. Given the opportunity for gainful employment, many of the men from the more remote islands remained in either the United States or Nassau, leaving the women and children and the older men to tend to the island farms. These residents could not cope with the heavy work of clearing, planting, and cleaning the fields and as a result many of the local farms were neglected, except for small subsistence farming, eliminating an important segment of the economy for these outer islands.

Given the considerable period of time the Contract was in effect and the large number of Bahamians who participated, the

---

62 D. Rolle, interviewed by Oral History team, College of The Bahamas, 1991, Thompson, Tracey L. "Remembering the Contract: Recollections of Bahamians," *The International Journal of Bahamian Studies,* accessed from http://journals.sfu.ca/cob/index.php/files/article/view/169/217, 18 June 2012.

arrangement had a significant social effect on the Bahamian population as well as the more obvious economic one: the decline of the nuclear family with a husband and wife and their children living under the same roof as a societal norm. Women comprised just under ten percent of Contract workers; by far the majority of workers were men. With absent male breadwinners, a culture began to emerge wherein women were thrust into responsibility as head of their households, and while some were able to cope and confidently shoulder this increased responsibility, others felt abandoned, hopeless, and lonely. With their husbands gone, some struck up intimate relationships with other men.

Moreover, many of the Contract workers who did not return home at the end of their contract period formally applied for permanent residency and even citizenship in the United States but there were others who jumped their contract and went underground, in some cases never returning to their families in The Bahamas.

Both of these groups integrated into American society, either by moving to Virginia, Central or North Florida, or into the coastal areas of Georgia and North and South Carolina, where they could pass off as African descendants called Gullahs (or Geechees), a term used to describe both the people and their language. The Gullah are known for their basket-weaving, an African skill shared by women in The Bahamas.

To this day, many communities in Florida and to a lesser extent in other southern states are populated by people of Bahamian origin who trace their U.S. status or residency to their Bahamian ancestors who were Contract workers.

Another social trend produced by Bahamian workers who had been on the Contract was the distinctive dress code which many of the men brought home with them. This consisted primarily in the acquisition of two garments, namely zoot suits and coveralls. The dressy zoot suit was usually reserved for attendance at Saturday night parties or at nightclubs like the Silver Slipper or Zanzibar where patrons danced the boogie-woogie or the jitterbug. The zoot suit, claimed to be influenced by American jazz and rhythm-and-blues artists, was a double-breasted suit with pleats and trousers very full at the knees but tapering down to pegs at the ankles, which always had cuffs. A long gold chain hung from a breast pocket on one side down across the chest and stomach, past the knee on the other side and back up that side to the lower vest pocket. Always worn with two-tone shoes and a wide hat, either felt or panama straw, the zoot suit became the uniform for a man's night on the town.

Coveralls were the casual attire worn by Contract returnees and comprised a pair of overalls worn with a pair of big, thick U.S. Army-issued boots called brogans, and usually topped off with some kind of headgear and bebop glasses. It should be noted that the Contract period coincided with the bebop era in American culture, when jazz was experiencing a change from the modified style to the more energized and improvised varieties.

The employment opportunities of the Contract lasted for more than twenty years, from 1943 to 1965. By the end of this period a total of over 30,000 Bahamians were employed by American farmers to work as farm laborers in over twenty states. Although the total amount of remittances is unknown, fewer than 5,000 Bahamians received a quarter of a million pounds from April 1943 to December 1944 alone.[63]

From the economic impact to a change in family mores to the more frivolous effect on fashion, the Contract and the Duke's personal involvement in the establishment and implementation of that agreement with the United States arguably had a most profound effect, positive and negative, on The Bahamas that was both immediate and enduring.

63 Lawlor, p. 259.

HARRY OAKES

The Bahamas' Greatest Benefactor?

L ong lines of voters queued up at several polling stations
in the area that was then the Western District of New
Providence to cast their votes for the candidate of their
choice in the by-election held in June 1938.

Sir Harry Oakes had been a resident of The Bahamas since
1934 when he gave up his Canadian residency to avoid exces-
sive tax impositions. At the time of the election, Oakes was visiting London with his wife, and did not even bother to return to
Nassau for the election or, indeed, even to campaign in person.
All of the usual campaign tactics, regarded as essential by political
combatants in any contest for elected office, were left in the charge
of his trusted "election generals," who for the most part, in the
local custom of the day, illegally compensated voters with money,
rum, or groceries to vote for their man. Hence, the election campaign slogan chanted by many: "We'll drink his rum, and have
some fun, and vote for Harry Oakes." Such payoffs could easily
be verified since there was no secret ballot in existence at that time

in The Bahamas; every qualified voter, as he presented himself to cast his ballot, had to openly declare to the polling officials the name of the candidate for whom he voted. It was an entirely male event, as women were neither allowed to vote nor to run for office.

Sir Harry did not remain a member of Parliament in the lower House for very long. In the following year he was elevated to the Legislative Council by the governor, Sir Charles Dundas. Appointments to this upper chamber were the sole prerogative of the governor under the colony's constitution at the time. Oakes's was largely a popular appointment among most sections of the local population, for Sir Harry continued to do much to encourage development and to bring the islands into the twentieth century.

He was born on December 23, 1874, in Sangerville, Maine, to a middle-class family. His father was a practicing surveyor and his mother a schoolteacher; they had two sons and three daughters. Oakes was short and stocky in build, merely five feet six inches tall, with a pugnacious jaw and a focused and determined look.

After an ordinary childhood upbringing and education, he achieved an undergraduate degree at Bowdoin College in Brunswick, Maine, and then spent two years at Syracuse Medical School while working part-time for the Carter Ink Company. At heart, however, he was an adventurer and explorer, with an aggressive and determined spirit; the tame life of a doctor would really not have suited him.

When he heard the news of gold finds in Alaska and the Yukon, he promptly quit medical school and set out on the long journey to find his fortune. In true fairy-tale fashion, he finally achieved that goal in 1916 in the Kirkland Lake district in northern Canada.

Up to this time Harry Oakes had retained his American citizenship; but in 1924, having by then been established as a full-time resident in Kirkland Lake, where he soon was known as its wealthiest and most benevolent resident, he became a Canadian citizen. That same year he went to Australia for a visit, and from there decided to take a cruise to South Africa to investigate gold production.

Aboard ship, he met a vivacious twenty-four-year-old woman, Eunice McIntyre, whose father was an Australian civil servant, on her way for a vacation visit with family members residing in South Africa. Although he was twice her age, the young woman's charm, good looks, and winning personality perfectly complemented his tough, retiring, and oft-times aggressive attitude. These opposite traits created a mutual attraction which led to a brief courtship after which they were married in her hometown of Sydney, Australia, in June of that same year.

They returned to Canada, where he bought a mansion near Niagara Falls for a half-million dollars, and then proceeded to remodel it in Tudor style to provide a matrimonial home. This was the first of several homes; in the years following he bought or built in Canada, London, Maine, Palm Beach, and The Bahamas.

Accompanying his vast financial successes were equally huge financial obligations in Canada, not the least of which was an annual tax bill of some three million dollars. He also generously responded to a constant stream of requests for contributions to various charities and fund-raisers, and regularly supported both the Liberal and Conservative political parties.

Since the need no longer existed for the daily hard work and drive which had propelled the past twenty-five years of his life, Oakes sought to replace some of the previous adventure and excitement by seeking national recognition. He was encouraged in this quest by the Liberal government of the day, which promised him a senate seat in return for a major contribution towards the upcoming election that year. However, the Conservative Party of Richard Bennett, who became prime minister, were the victors at the polls and, being aware of Oakes's support for the Liberals, vindictively put in place a levy which required him to pay a tax of $250,000 on the value of land and parks in Niagara Falls which he had already given to the nation. Although his philanthropy was greatly appreciated in Niagara Falls, he continued to have tax problems with the national government.

When the minister of mines called to advise him that a higher tax was being contemplated on large gold mines, Oakes felt that this was the last straw, and he thereupon moved from Canada to The Bahamas. The media in Canada did not respond well to his leaving Canada, and printed critical stories with headlines reading "Multi-Millionaire Champ Tax Dodger" and "Santa Claus to The Bahamas but Heart like Frigidaire to the Land that Gave Him Wealth." Many politicians, however, condemned the government for driving away such a prominent and generous citizen.

Canada's loss was The Bahamas' gain. Indeed, the local government of the day regarded it as such a windfall that Oakes had decided to transfer his residential status to The Bahamas, with all the resulting benefits that would surely flow from his generous penchant for development, for property acquisition, and for his well-known benevolence, that every effort and enticement were used, in every influential quarter, to secure his permanent loyalty to The Bahamas. These initiatives emanated from positions as high as the governor of the colony, Sir Bede Clifford.

Sir Bede had learned that one of the reasons for Oakes's disenchantment with his domicile in Canada was the fact that he had sought to cap his growing role as an outstanding Canadian citizen by being nominated for the award of a British title of honour, and to this end had become one of the largest financial contributors to both national political parties in Canada. The disappointment of not receiving a knighthood together with the increased imposition of taxes were the main factors which drove him in disgust to turn his back on Canada and take up residence in The Bahamas.

Harold Christie, a leading Bahamian real estate businessman who was well connected in upper echelons of The Bahamas, immediately developed Oakes as a primary customer to whom he sold thousands of acres of prime Bahamian real estate, leading to a close friendship between the two men.

Sir Bede also set out without delay to promote Oakes's social and political ascendancy in the local community. Official correspondence in the Colonial Office files from Governor Bede Clifford to Sir John Maffey in the Colonial Office in London is most revealing. A memorandum dated January 13, 1937, seeks to obtain two "nearly-impossible-to-obtain" seats for Oakes and his wife to attend and view the coronation of King George VI later that year, a request that was approved.

Although this could be considered a social favour, the memorandum is also a glaring instance of an attempt at an official bribe. In order to secure Oakes's commitment for generous contributions and involvement in development and beautification projects in The Bahamas, Sir Bede blatantly also requested that Oakes be considered for an appointment which would carry a title of honour that he so very much desired. The tone and content of the memorandum clearly and unashamedly show Sir Bede's intent. It states:

"You have no doubt heard of Mr. Harry Oakes of Canada, who is reputed to be one of the wealthiest men in the world and is said to receive an income from his Canadian mines which can most conveniently be compared with the interest on the National Debt.

"It would appear that my friend 'Mitch' Hepburn, Premier of Ontario, has been extorting money from wealthy Canadians in a way that would make even HM Commissioners of Revenue blush, including retrospective taxation on a grand scale. Anyhow, it appears that Mr. Oakes had been very public spirited and had made some generous gifts to the Dominion, but was finally so harassed that he shook the Canadian dust from his shoes, and now divides his time between England, The Bahamas and Florida. He has bought about an eighth of the island of New Providence, and has been a great benefactor to the Colony."[64]

An eighth of the island of New Providence is a vast expanse of land; this was then, as now, the principal island in the Bahamian group. Nassau, situated on this island, is the capital of the nation and remains the centre of government, commerce, higher education, tourism, and population, even to this day. To own this amount of land in the capital island gave Oakes tremendous status and influence in this developing country.

In his letter to the Colonial Office in London the governor continued to expand on the steps that should be taken in order to secure this powerful man's loyalty, the benefits that The Bahamas might receive from his favour, and the political response to such action:

"My own impression is that, having cut himself adrift from Canada, he feels as though he has no definite Country, and is looking round with a view to make some place his official domicile.

"It is my opinion that, given a little encouragement, he would make The Bahamas his domicile as he has already built himself a big house here.

It has occurred to me that if he was given a place on the Executive or Legislative Council which carries with it the title 'Honourable,' he would permanently identify himself with this Colony and make handsome contributions towards developing and beautifying it,

---

64 B. Clifford, Sir, to Sir John Maffey, *Colonial Office Papers CO23/580/8,* Bahamas Department of Archives, 13 January 1937.

particularly as he has already done a great deal in this direction without any encouragement. Any such appointment might momentarily create a little jealousy amongst local politicians, but as nearly all those who have shown any interest in the Colony that was not personal or remunerative are already members of the Legislative or Executive Councils, any such reaction would not be shared by the community at large, who would, I think, welcome Mr. Oakes in their midst. Before taking any action, however, I should welcome an expression of your views and, if you are favourably inclined, I would consult Members of Council before coming to a decision.

"As I have said, Oakes has been a great benefactor to this Colony, and he has asked me if I could do anything to assist him and his wife in regard to the Coronation.

"While I believe that properly handled this place has a great future, I am conscious of the precarious nature of its tourist revenue, and I am now busy trying to encourage capitalists such as Oakes to develop such resources as it possesses, and I feel sure that Oakes would lend money at extremely low rates of interest for such enterprises as Harbour Development if he were sentimentally attached to the place.

"I should therefore be most obliged for anything you and Bromley could do to give Mr. and Mrs. Oakes a good view of the Coronation. Please forgive me importuning you in this way, but I can assure you that my motives are inspired solely by the desire to promote the welfare of a British Colony."[65]

Following this communication, Governor Clifford considered it best to elevate Harry Oakes gradually, and on March 9, 1937,

65 B. Clifford, Sir, to Sir John Maffey, *Colonial Office Papers CO23/580/8*, 13 January 1937.

began this process by appointing him a member of the local Board of Public Works and also a justice of the peace.[66] Ten days later, the governor was able to report to the Colonial Office in London that the effect of these appointments was "already noticeable in that he has begun at his own expense, and without inspiration from any source, to build a public road of considerable importance, and I think he will purchase and reclaim one of our worst swamps."[67]

Like the Duke of Windsor, Governor Bede Clifford was married to an American and was quite pro-American in his policies and attitude. In one of his reports to the Colonial Office he cited a number of U.S. citizens who had acquired property and business interests in The Bahamas, and he recommended that it would be in the best interests of the Colony "to facilitate the naturalization of the better class of American families"[68] who not only had a residence, but also a business in The Bahamas and who he thought would welcome the prospects of being allowed to become British subjects.

This policy had considerable risks and Sir Bede recognized this. In a memorandum he wrote to Sir William Ormsby-Gore, the secretary of state for the colonies, he cautioned that a possible danger in implementing such a policy was the possibility that any considerable influx of wealthy aliens might lead to their being inspired to attempt to control the government, as was the historic case in South Africa with the attempt of the Transvaal Uitlanders. He pointed out that in the political climate of the time,

---

66 B. Clifford, Sir, to Sir John Maffey, *Colonial Office Papers CO23/580/5*, 9 March 1937.

67 B. Clifford, Sir, to Sir John Maffey, *Colonial Office Papers CO23/580/10*, 23 January 1937.

68 B. Clifford, Sir, to Sir Ormsby Gore, *Colonial Office Papers CO23/580/8*, 13 January 1937.

the outcome of elections to the House of Assembly could be determined by the expenditure of a relatively small sum—just a few hundred pounds. He concludes, however, that, "On the other hand, the better class American could, I believe, become useful and helpful members of society, and staunch supporters [sic] of British ideals and British Institutions."[69]

It was during this pro-foreign atmosphere set by official colonial thinking at the top, that on June 8, 1939, Harry Oakes was conferred a baronetcy, a hereditary British title of honour, to become Sir Harry Oakes, baronet (or Bt.). Upon his untimely death at age sixty-eight, on July 7, 1943, the baronetcy passed to his eldest son, the late Sir Sydney Oakes, whose life ended at age thirty-nine in a fatal motor accident in Nassau on August 8, 1966; he was succeeded by his son, who became Sir Christopher Oakes, Bt.

From his arrival in The Bahamas to take up permanent residence in 1934, until his death in 1943, Sir Harry Oakes arguably did more than any other person, agency, or government to affect life positively in The Bahamas. His deep imprint on the development of New Providence and its capital city, Nassau, is still much in evidence three-quarters of a century later. When he left Canada, he already owned two residential properties in The Bahamas, one called the Caves Estate, situated on a hilltop site immediately south of a famous geological novelty known as the Caves and overlooking Lake Killarney, and the other, which was a sprawling, luxurious multiroom, two-story mansion called Westbourne situated on the waterfront at Cable Beach, and being the site of what is now known as SuperClubs Breezes Bahamas.

69 B. Clifford, Sir, to Sir Ormsby Gore, *Colonial Office Papers CO23/580/8*, 13 January 1937.

With his ownership of huge tracts of land in New Providence alone, and with the same energy and enthusiasm that propelled his relentless drive as a gold prospector in the past, Oakes set about land developing, earth clearing, landscaping, sheep farming, and other ambitious projects in which he invested approximately half a million pounds, a huge sum even today.

These ventures not only enhanced his real estate holdings, but also gave employment to more than 1,500 Bahamians—skilled workers and labourers who, prior to his arrival, were having great difficulty in eking out a living in an era of economic hardship.

One of the major developments established by Sir Harry is located south of the southern borders of the city limits in the area west of Baillou Hill Road and Big Pond and to the north of the Baillou Hill Range. He acquired this property and developed it as a private airfield, which soon after was expanded and utilized as an air base during World War II. It later became the country's first international airport and was named Oakes Airport. This facility was subsequently acquired by the Bahamian government. After the development of Windsor Field, the country's present international airport in the Western District, Oakes Airport was redeveloped by the government and renamed the Queen Elizabeth Sports Centre. This complex is today the site of a national sports complex with a 15,000-seat national stadium, a gymnasium, a training track and field stadium, an Olympic-size fully equipped swimming complex, tennis centre, baseball and softball fields, a nearby government high school, and other government offices and facilities. Near Westbourne Sir Harry cleared and built a magnificent golf course, totally redeveloped as the TPC Golf Course at Baha Mar.

Of all of Oakes's property acquisitions in Nassau, perhaps none was more important than his purchase of the historic downtown New Colonial Hotel, which he renovated and renamed the British Colonial Hotel. A popular local anecdote, if legend be true, claims that Oakes was annoyed after being denied admittance or served badly one day when he appeared in the hotel's restaurant seemingly inappropriately dressed (his daily custom being to dress in high leather boots and his prospector's garb). He is said to have immediately gone onto Bay Street to the law office of his attorney, Sir Kenneth Solomon, and arranged to purchase the hotel. He then returned to the establishment the following day for the explicit purpose of firing the staff member who had insulted him.

The hotel remained in the family ownership until the early years of the present century when his youngest and only surviving son, Harry P. Oakes, sold the property to Canadian investor Ron Kelly together with funding from a pension fund which, after effecting considerable renovations, operated the hotel as the British Colonial Hilton. The hotel property was sold in 2014 to the China State Construction Engineering Corporation.

Oakes's purchase of this property demonstrated his constant desire for continuing development in The Bahamas, and in like measure the improvement it created also reflected the increase of his personal economic wealth. For example, he imported from Britain the island's first big-city modern passenger bus, which he used to transport his many workers from their homes Over the Hill to their jobs on his several projects in the Western District of the Island. As a generous benefit to the local over-the-hill residents his buses were used on Sunday afternoons to provide bus rides for their enjoyment and tours of the Western District. The author well remembers an occasion, one Sunday afternoon, when as a young boy he was taken, along with a group of his friends and neighbours, on a free bus ride to view the Oakes development then in progress. This bus service in fact became the origin of what has today developed into a large jitney bus service which traverses all the main residential districts and city area of the island of New Providence.

As an elected representative, Oakes became attached to Gambier Village, which historically was the oldest settlement in New Providence. It is a quaint native village located in the northwestern section of the island of New Providence. As part of the electoral Western District, which formed part of Sir Harry's constituency and thereby fell under his political responsibility, he virtually adopted the village and its residents and personally contributed from his own finances to its upkeep and its people. Even as late as half a century after Sir Harry's death a memorial photograph which was donated to the school in the village was still hanging in the schoolhouse, reminding residents of his generosity and interest in their welfare.

His vast investments and ownership in the various landholds and enterprises greatly enhanced the development and economic growth of the islands, especially during the period preceding and during World War II when investment opportunities came almost to a halt.

Sadly, Sir Harry Oakes's entrepreneurial and generous influence in The Bahamas, and his ascendancy to a title he had sought for so long, was not to last for very much longer.

During the early morning of Thursday, July 8, 1943, the bludgeoned and burnt body of Sir Harry Oakes was discovered by Harold Christie, later Sir Harold Christie, his close friend and companion of Sir Harry in Westbourne, a palatial country house adjoining the Bahamas Country Club, which was but one of several large estates owned by him in Nassau and the Out Islands of The Bahamas. The investigation revealed that numerous fires had been set around the room. What followed the events of that morning gave rise to one of the world's most celebrated murder cases, still classified as unsolved.

Two Miami police officers, Captain E. W. Melchen and Captain James O. Barker, were asked by the Duke to come to Nassau to help with the investigation. This was motivated by the Duke's lack of confidence in the ability of the local police officers, who with the sole exception of the commissioner were native Bahamians. Captain Melchen had previously met the Duke and Duchess when he was assigned to guard them on their visits to Miami. On learning of the tragic death of Sir Harry Oakes, the Duke cancelled all his appointments so that he might lend his personal assistance in the investigations. As it happened neither of two Miami police officers had any previous experience in homicide investigations and, indeed, one of the officers later was accused of falsifying evidence in this case.

The first suspect was Harold Christie, who had spent the night with Sir Harry in an adjoining room at Westbourne in preparation for a trip they proposed making the next morning. It seemed unavoidable that Mr. Christie would easily have been awakened by the noise that would have accompanied the horrendous attacks on Sir Harry had he really been in the adjoining room at the time. This gave credence to the evidence given at the trial by Captain Edward Sears, a Bahamian police officer, who testified that he saw Mr. Christie driving into the downtown area of the city in the late-night hours at the relevant time. Later information disclosed that he was in fact visiting a female friend with whom he spent part of the night. It is therefore not surprising that later evidence also revealed that Captain James Barker examined Mr. Christie for skin or hair burns on his body, especially his hands and head; he found him unscathed and free of any signs of burn marks, chars, or singes that might have linked him to the murder.

Sir Harry Oakes's son-in-law, Count Marie Alfred Fouquereaux de Marigny, who had earlier secretly married the Oakes's teen-aged daughter, Nancy, was also physically examined. He was suspected because he and Sir Harry were known to very much dislike each other after de Marigny's marriage to Oakes's young daughter.

It was discovered that he had burns on his hands and arms, and singed hair on his head, eyebrows, and perhaps his beard. The explanation that he gave attributed the hair burns as mainly due to cleaning chickens over open fires at his chicken farm. After extensive police investigations, however, Count de Marigny was arrested on the afternoon of the next day, July 9, 1943, and charged with the murder. His trial began on October 18, 1943, and was completed in November 1943.

De Marigny was a French descendant and was born in Mauritius, a British island colony off the coast of South Africa. He came to Nassau several years before the murder and owned properties in New Providence, where he had his residence, and on Eleuthera, where he developed farms.

De Marigny was represented by well-known Bahamian counsel, Godfrey Higgs, and assisted by Ernest Callender, as junior counsel. The prosecution was led by A. F. Adderley, an outstanding local Bahamian counsel who was briefed by the attorney general. Hearing the case was Chief Justice Sir Oscar Daly.

After a world-famous trial, attracting internationally known journalists, criminologists, and other legal experts, de Marigny was acquitted, but following a strange caveat attached by the jury to their verdict, he was ordered to be deported from The Bahamas as an undesirable. Accordingly, accompanied by his young wife Nancy, he left Nassau for Cuba shortly after his acquittal.

Among the many criticisms that have been made concerning the handling of the Oakes murder case, several have been levelled as interference by the Duke of Windsor himself. One of these was the transfer of the commissioner of police, Colonel Erskine-Lindop, who was sent to Trinidad as deputy commissioner of police immediately after the investigation of the murder began. This transfer was made at the insistence of the Duke ostensibly in order to accommodate his appointment of the two Miami police officers without causing any undue embarrassment to Erskine-Lindop. A minute in the confidential files of the Colonial Office in England, made by an under-secretary, T. K. Lloyd, states that he generally agrees that "it was largely at the insistence of H.R.H. that we moved Lindop and landed Trinidad with a problem."[70] Another Colonial Office file also discloses an enlightening communication on the same issue dated March 8, 1944, written by the Duke to the secretary of state for the colonies, Oliver Stanley, as follows:

"Dear Oliver,
As a member of the Royal Family, I have since childhood been taught to avoid politics like the plague, and as a brother of the King, it would not only be unfortunate but undesirable were I to become involved in a highly contentious political conflict which is fundamentally a racial one. The Bahamas do not consider themselves part of the West Indies. Lindop is now second in command in Trinidad. Lt. Col. Lancaster has been here for 3 months and has already tightened up the Police Force.
"A Commission of Enquiry was organized to tighten up the Police Force . . . they are now trained for crime detection and equipment. It was the lack of training of the local CID that caused me to call in the American Detectives . . . their ignorance of the British Criminal Law allowed the serious breakdown in the evidence against de Marigny. The Colony is literally running on a shoestring. I purposely absented myself and the Duchess from the Colony during the de Marigny trial to avoid adverse publicity. I didn't want to be dragged into sordid and vulgar daily newspaper reports . . . there was a morbid interest in America."[71]

70 T. K. Lloyd, Minute, *Colonial Office Papers CO23/785/7*, Bahamas Department of Archives, 30 May 1945.

71 Duke of Windsor to Oliver Stanley, *Colonial Office Papers CO23/967/126*,

There were other commentators of the period, however, who held a different view of the Duke's interference with the investigation, including this arbitrary arrangement to remove Colonel Erskine-Lindop from The Bahamas so as to provide a free hand for the two detectives imported from Miami.

The consistently outspoken editor of *The Tribune*, Sir Etienne Dupuch, wrote the following in an article in 1974, which was reprinted and amended in 1983:

"Colonel Lindop is a friend of mine, close enough to be the godfather of my son, Pierre. In 1951, I passed through Trinidad on my way to an Inter American Press Association Conference in Montevideo, Uruguay. In Trinidad I spent an evening with the Colonel. 'De Marigny was an unprincipled rascal,' Colonel Lindop told me, 'but he did not kill Oakes. My investigations had just reached the point where, during the interrogation of a possible suspect, I extracted information that I am sure was a clue to the murderer or his accomplice when the case was taken out of my hands. I was transferred to Trinidad and was not asked to give evidence at the trial.'"[72]

The acquittal of de Marigny was very embarrassing for the Duke, as the royal governor did not want his legacy to include such a high-profile and internationally publicized murder remaining unsolved.

The murder of Sir Harry Oakes will forever be remembered as one of the infamous crimes of the century which marred the Windsor years in The Bahamas. Sir Harry's positive impact on

8 March 1944.

72 E. Dupuch, Editorial, *Nassau Daily Tribune*, 26 August 1974, p. 9. Reprinted, 1983.

the development of The Bahamas left residents from all sectors of the society feeling a strong sense of gratitude to this great benefactor, and providing a suitable tribute to his memory was a prevalent topic of discussion for many months after his death. These sentiments were not lost on the Duke and he took the lead in putting talk into action by inviting the Honorable A. K. Solomon on January 24, 1944, to become chairman of the Oakes Memorial Committee, which would consider the most suitable form of establishing a lasting tribute to Sir Harry.

One of the committee's recommendations, successfully realized, was the erection of a memorial column within the triangle immediately opposite the Pan American Airways building at the northern entrance to Oakes Field, where it remains today, providing a permanent reminder of this friend of The Bahamas.

Sir Harry Oakes moved in the social circles of the Duke of Windsor, and had regular contact and influence with him. While his murder remains an unsolved mystery, the involvement and interaction of the Duke leaves many unanswered questions.

PART 3

HIS LEGACY

THE FIRST LADY

For most of the duration of World War II, the Duchess of Windsor served prominently as the First Lady of the Bahama Islands, playing a leading and an outstanding role in many ways.

Immediately after their arrival in Nassau, the Duchess found herself involved in various official as well as social functions. The Bahamas Branch of the British Red Cross Society and the local branch of the Imperial Order of the Daughters of the Empire were parts of two British international organizations of which she automatically became president and honorary president, respectively, by virtue of her marital status. Serving in this capacity at a time when Great Britain was fully involved at the height of World War II, in Europe and the Middle East, the offices she occupied were thus more than mere token posts and required actual duties that increasingly occupied her time. She not only involved herself fully in the activities of these organizations, but also volunteered at a military canteen established for foreign officers and airmen based in The Bahamas that was located in a prominent building formerly housing the Bahamian Club which, prior to the war, was a well-known licensed gambling casino.

Shortly after the outbreak of the war, The Bahamas was utilized by the Allies as the location for a training base for airmen, with a large airfield, named Windsor Field for the new Royal Governor, constructed on the undeveloped western end of the island. The airfield was usable by the end of the summer of 1940, by which time some 4,000 officers and airmen were stationed there in connection with the training program established by the RAF Coastal Command together with the U.S. Army and Air Force.

Given the increased number of troops and the ongoing demands of the world war, the war service which the Duchess provided as First Lady was especially notable, including instances when survivors from tankers and other ships sunk by enemy submarines that preyed on vessels in the Caribbean and off the Florida Coast, landed in Nassau and needed assistance. Indeed, the Duchess herself takes credit in her autobiography, *The Heart Has Its Reasons*, for her full involvement in the war effort, when she declares that she

> "scarcely had a spare moment . . . every morning at the Red Cross, from nine o'clock until noon; each afternoon at the Canteen. Here I did a little of everything; but I found that my real talent was as a short-order cook. I never kept track of the number of orders of bacon and eggs that I served up, but on the basis of forty an afternoon, and three hundred and sixty-five afternoons a year for nearly three years I arrived at a rough total of about forty thousand. And that's a lot of eggs."[73]

---

73 Windsor, Wallis Warfield, Duchess of, *The Heart Has Its Reasons*, London, The Companion Book Club Odhams Press, 1958, p. 355.

The Duchess is also remembered to this day for her identification with the increased quality of island life by her having established two infant-welfare clinics for the care of expectant mothers and young children. The first, formerly called The Duchess of Windsor Clinic but now known as the Blue Hill Road Clinic, is located at the foot of the hill in Grant's Town, just below the Government House complex; the other clinic, recently closed, was called the Bilney Lane Children's Home. These clinics served the native residents of the southern, western, and eastern districts of New Providence and were maintained and operated as an adjunct to the government owned and operated public hospital, the Princess Margaret Hospital. The Blue Hill Road Clinic has in recent years been enlarged and continues to serve as a valuable and busy outlying subsidiary to the main hospital.

Despite her commitment to help the British and Allied troops stationed in The Bahamas, and her efforts to improve medical conditions on the island, the Duchess never warmed up to the country and its people. Her candid negative sentiments are found in letters sent to her favorite aunt, Mrs. Bessie Merryman of Baltimore, Maryland, who throughout her life remained her friend and confidante and with whom she shared many intimate confidences over the five-year period that the Duchess lived in the island nation. Their correspondence provides an insight into the true feelings of dislike, and even disgust, which the Duchess felt about her stay in The Bahamas—a stark contrast to her public expressions of happiness, gratification, and approval.

The fact is that from the beginning, the Duchess approached the appointment of her husband to the governorship of The Bahamas with derision. Both the Duke and the Duchess were embittered by what they considered their unfair lot, but to improve their situation, to rise back up the chain of power and prestige, they had to *appear* to embrace the Bahama mission. En route to this new assignment, she wrote to her Aunt Bessie on August 7, 1940, stating, "Naturally we loathe the job, but it was the only way out of a difficult situation—as we did not want to return to England except under our own conditions."[74]

This attitude was coloured, no doubt, by her resentment of the Royal Family and the British officials who had essentially forced them to accept a position in a country considered by many to be an inconsequential outpost of the British Empire. Given these circumstances, it is certainly plausible that the royal couple viewed their new domicile as banishment and exile, rather than a tropical escape from a world at war.

In 1940, after the Duchess arrived in Nassau with her royal husband, she showed no change of heart from the scorn she displayed after learning of the Duke's appointment. In a letter to her Aunt Bessie written soon after their arrival in Nassau, she described The Bahamas as their Elba,[75] attempting to dramatize the Duke's appointment as akin to Napoleon's island exile after he temporarily abdicated in 1814. Her historical allusion would have been more accurate had she referred instead to the island of St. Helena, the small British crown colony off the West Coast of Africa. It was there that the victorious British banished Napoleon in 1815 after he had returned to France from Elba to attack his European neighbors but was defeated at Waterloo by the Duke of Marlborough. Writing to her Aunt Bessie again just two months later, the Duchess further reported that "things are going slowly here and I am not interested enough to push very hard."[76]

---

74 Bloch, p. 103.

75 Martin, p. 411.

76 Bloch, p. 144.

The fact is that she hated Nassau and constantly complained about the oppressive heat, her contempt for the "natives," the confinement of living in a small community, and the reduced quality of life as compared with the opulence and glamour of major cities like London and Paris where she was accustomed to the company of royalty and high society.

In her autobiography she refers to the royal couple's posting in The Bahamas as "five fruitful years," and says that "our lives in Nassau had been happy and imbued with a sense of purpose that we were sorry to lose."[77] Contrary to these public statements, however, it is believed that the Duchess of Windsor never overcame her intensely negative attitude towards The Bahamas.

The Duke had expressed equally negative sentiments about his appointment and tenure in The Bahamas, but regardless of the royal couple's mutual feelings or even their motivations for doing so, each set about establishing positive roles for themselves throughout their stay, which served to benefit the islands and its people.

77 Duchess of Windsor, pp. 346 and 360.

THE ROYAL GOVERNOR

On balance, the Windsor years in The Bahamas, for the Duke as governor and his Duchess as First Lady, as well as for the Bahamian nation generally, were not successful by any measure. As the firstborn son of the king of England, he had been entitled in his youth to be recognized for his privileged position as Prince of Wales and, accordingly, as the future king of England. This provided him with widespread exposure to the privileges and functions of this high office, and also a personal awareness of the current political era, which was then emerging amongst colonial subjects throughout the British Empire.

This valuable experience was acquired firsthand from his travels across the globe, from which he gained a reputation as a highly effective and popular royal ambassador. Yet, his personal attitude of superiority, together with his constant display of class prejudice and obvious ingrained bigotry against labourers and blacks, exposed his true nature as a racist.

After renouncing the throne of England, the only other job he ever held was the appointment in 1940 as the governor and commander in chief of the Bahama Islands. When the Duke arrived in The Bahamas in August 1940 to assume the post as governor, the entire archipelago was suffering from the injustices and indignities constantly experienced by the eighty-five-percent black majority of the native population. Many existing inequities cried out for change: the limited voting system, which was based on a property ownership qualification; the disenfranchisement of Bahamian women, and the absence of a suffrage movement; the imbalance in the rate of wages; the problems with inadequate education, housing, and land ownership for the masses; the appalling race relations with its open policy of colour discrimination in public places; racial prejudice in the civil service; and the racial bigotry, which was openly displayed in public places, in employment practices in government, in the banks, in professional offices, and in many commercial shops in the city.

When the Duke left The Bahamas after five years as royal governor, every one of those inequities remained just as he had found them. Despite his special qualifications and exceptional influence, which would certainly have enabled him to initiate and achieve change in many of those degrading conditions, he was content to allow the status quo to continue. As governor he possessed certain constitutional powers, especially with regard to releasing financial expenditures voted by the House of Assembly, which, in addition to his special influence with the Colonial Office, could have resulted in his successfully overriding the wishes and bigotry of the white business oligarchy in The Bahamas known as "the Bay Street Boys." He certainly could have achieved many social improvements and physical developments had he so wished. However, by maintaining members of the Bay Street group as his advisors and social circle, he deliberately chose not to include black Bahamians in any position of governance or to take steps that would have produced, if for no other humanitarian reason, better race relations and harmony.

In retrospect, this ought not to be thought surprising as race relations in the first half of the twentieth century had not yet generally begun the move toward equality in civil rights as evidenced internationally today; and the Duke himself was certainly no exception to the prevalent way of thinking. Indeed, he had approached the job with a negative attitude from the start, and both he and the Duchess commenced the appointment with loathing instead of a sense of purpose.

The infamous Bay Street Riot of 1942 was a clear warning to the Duke that all was not well with the majority of the population. Although the eruption was triggered by the inequity in wages paid to local workers employed at the ongoing Project development in the Western District, the immediate aftermath of that explosive incident, including the cries of many of the black leadership, such as Dr. C. R. Walker's emotional address to the Duke just five days after the riot, should have been an immediate call to action for the Duke to address the appalling political, social, and economic conditions of the masses. But he failed to act.

At the opening of Parliament following the riots, the Duke in his "speech from the throne" did indeed tell the legislators that there was need for a drastic change in the psychology both of the legislators and the people whom they represented. He said the Out Island representatives particularly, as well as their inhabitants, had to change their way of thinking in order to enable them to keep up with the evolving times particularly with regard to social development and well-being.[78] However, his quest for reform was somewhat facile, as the House of Parliament did not vote the funds

78 Bloch, p. 275.

necessary to finance his recommended projects and he chose not to use his gubernatorial influence to force a change.

It was speeches such as this that gave the appearance of progressive thought, but with no follow-up, his words ultimately proved to be empty promises. In fact, the Duke and his advisors later made only a slight adjustment to the wage scale of the labourers employed on the Project.

It was only after the General Strike of 1958, sixteen years later, that more far-reaching reforms and improvements were addressed: hotel workers, stevedores, and others similarly employed became unionized; legislation was passed to allow for fair labour standards including collective bargaining; the franchise was granted to women; the incongruous "company vote" in elections was abolished; a redistribution of seats for membership in the House of Assembly was put in place; the life of the House of Assembly was reduced from seven to five years; and legislation was passed requiring that all elections in all the islands in the colony were to be held on the same day. Not one of these political or social reforms was ever considered by the Duke as urgently necessary, and certainly never initiated by him.

And so, what manner of man was he?

He was weak.

Even though constitutionally the governor had "reserved powers" over financial measures, which could be used as powerful political leverage in overcoming the objections of the House of Assembly, he never pushed for much-needed reforms whenever such measures were opposed by the Bay Street power base, even when these changes were being sought by the Colonial Office in London. Above all, the Duke desired a restoration of his own status, or a semblance of same—a more prestigious ambassadorial posting to America or Canada, something worthy of a former king of England. Upsetting the apple cart in The Bahamas might well have jeopardized his chances. That it turned out he was awarded no higher posting, that he squandered his only opportunity to leave a lasting positive legacy is both tragic for the Duke—and educational for others.

He was prejudiced.

Although his political objectives as governor of The Bahamas were often well intentioned, he chose to confine his social and advisory circle strictly to members of the white oligarchy of Bay Street.

He was a racist.

Numerous incidents throughout his stay in The Bahamas demonstrated that the Duke regarded black Bahamians as second-class citizens. During his entire period in office no black person was ever invited to Government House socially; indeed, staff members of the period have reported that not once did a black Bahamian of either high or low estate enter the front door of Government House during the Duke's governorship. There were a few non-white politicians, professional persons, volunteers departing for war service, and others who had occasion to call on the governor; however, on those occasions when a "coloured" official or visitor had to be received at Government House, the meeting was always arranged in the adjoining ballroom, on the outside patio adjoining the governor's office, or outside in the gardens.

Colour prejudice was also demonstrated in the Duke's personal correspondence, such as in a letter written by him on July 26, 1941, to the secretary of state for the colonies, Lord Moyne.

The Duke stated in this letter that that he was "well aware that the official colour bar does not exist in the other West Indian Colonies; indeed, I well remember coloured members of the Legislature being present on all official occasions during my visits as Prince of Wales."[79]

79 Bloch, p. 195.

However, in that same letter he attempts to justify the great difference in The Bahamas, calling it a "colour problem" which he states was due to "their close proximity to the mainland of America, [presumably white Bahamian residents] still maintain a very staunch and American attitude towards the colour problem, and white Bahamians will not allow their wives to sit down to dinner with coloured people."[80]

He then confirms his own acceptance of such prejudice by stating, "No one in their right senses would ever be so tactless as to invite coloured people to meet American guests at dinner."[81]

His letter ends with his choice to simply allow the status quo, stating that "this problem . . . is one that will have to be tackled sooner or later[.] I am quite sure it is 'a fence that must not be rushed' in The Bahamas."[82]

He never made any attempt to deal with racial inequality during his term of office in The Bahamas.

He was disloyal.

Some writers have even described him as a traitor. Certainly, the confirmed reports of his pro-Nazi leanings, including his much publicized visit to Adolf Hitler in 1938, prior to the outbreak of World War II, and his illegal financial and currency exchange dealings, which were clearly prohibited by wartime exchange control regulations, all raise legitimate questions as to his loyalty and to the genuineness of his support of the war effort. It is inconceivable that this former king of England, and the current governor and commander in chief of a British colony during a time when England was at war with Germany, could have engaged in

80 Bloch, p. 195.

81 Ibid.

82 Ibid.

such subversive activity that it caused him to be the subject of constant surveillance by the American FBI.

The Duke made such insensitive commentary that Fulton Oursler, Sr., editor in chief of *Liberty* magazine, reported it to President Roosevelt. In 1940 the Duke was interviewed by Oursler. After the death of his father in 1952, Fulton Oursler, Jr., was interviewed in an article in the December issue of the *American Heritage* magazine in which he disclosed previously unpublished notes left by his father related to his 1940 interview with the Duke. Oursler Sr. felt the Duke made "near treasonous" statements when he described rumors that the Italian defeat in Greece might lead to a revolution in Germany as "too much wishful thinking; that there would be no revolution in Germany, and that it would be a tragic thing for the world if Hitler were overthrown."[83] The Duke also told Oursler that Hitler was not ony the right and logical leader of the German people, he was also a great man.[84]

Following the Burma Street Riot, when the Bahamian nation and its people were in turmoil, Dr. C. R. Walker posed a direct question at the end of his stirring address to The Duke of Windsor in his role as governor general of The Bahamas:

"Art thou he that cometh?"

The unfortunate answer is a resounding *No!*

83 Bloch, pp. 177–178.

84 Ibid.

EPILOGUE

THE DEPARTURE

On Sunday, April 29, 1945, the Duke broadcast his formal farewell speech to the people of The Bahamas over Radio Station ZNS, which was the only broadcasting system in operation in the colony at that time. No other festivities or celebrations were scheduled for the general population. The governor began his address at 12:45 p.m. on that afternoon— the seemingly genuine, warm, and friendly tone of his voice resounding over the airwaves. The text of his speech was not long, and he began as follows:

"This is going to be the shortest broadcast you have ever heard me make, for when one feels something deeply, words seem superfluous. But as the Duchess and I will be leaving Nassau very soon now, we did not wish to go away without saying goodbye to you all. For the Colony, our departure merely marks the end of another administration; but for us it is the closing of an interesting, happy chapter in our lives. I use the word 'happy' purposely. Although there have been many grim and anxious periods during the five years we have spent here working with you, and we have all been very conscious of the death, suffering and destruction that is still being endured by the Allied Forces on all Fronts, by the people of Britain, and by countless millions in Countries that have been occupied by the enemy—the Duchess and I have been very happy here.

"Our regret at leaving, therefore, is very real; and we are going to miss the life of Nassau, and our official duties, as we are going to miss our friends and all that The Bahamas has to offer. So you can be sure that you have by no means seen the last of us, and that we shall always look forward to returning to these Islands which we have learned to know and love so well.

"That the Duchess and I will always follow your fortunes with the keenest interest goes without saying; for how could we do otherwise after so long and intimate an association with all your activities. You are of course going to have your post-war problems like all other Countries, but I am confident that you are going to be equal to the task of solving them.

"The Duchess wants to add a personal message of her own and will now speak to you."[85]

During their five-year stay in The Bahamas the Duchess made few public speeches. One of those rare occasions was during this farewell address by the Duke; when she spoke, brief though it was, it was with great grace and a similar air of authenticity as the Duke:

"Although the Duke is really speaking for both of us, I do want you to know how very sad I am to think that soon the last of the

---

85 E. Dupuch, "Report of Farewell Broadcast of Duke of Windsor," *Nassau Daily Tribune*, 30 April 1945.

Islands of The Bahamas will be receding from my view below the horizon.

"It has been a very happy time that the Duke and I have spent amongst you, and a pleasure for me to have been able to contribute, in a small way, to the war effort of the women of the Colony, whose loyal devotion and enthusiasm has been an inspiration, and made my work with them so easy.

"I hope that it will not be too long before we can see you all again, and until then, 'Au Revoir.' "[86]

The Duchess then returned to her seat, and the Duke resumed his farewell broadcast with these concluding words:

"In saying 'Au Revoir,' we wish you the best of luck, with the hope that the coming years will bring you everything you desire.

"God Bless You All."[87]

It is interesting to note the manner in which both the Duke and Duchess separately addressed their farewell greetings to the people of The Bahamas. Neither offered even a remote indication of their true discontent with this period of enforced "exile" in this small nation. This was quite in contrast to the comments made by the Duchess to her Aunt Bessie when they were first appointed and were residing in The Bahamas; only in such correspondence did the Duchess disclose her true feelings of disdain for The Bahamas and its people.

Up until the very end of their stay, the royal couple not only publically maintained their royal demeanour but also displayed their

---

86 E. Dupuch, "Report of Farewell Broadcast of Duchess of Windsor," *Nassau Daily Tribune*, 30 April 1945.

87 Ibid.

haughty attitude towards the Bahamian people. A good example is that in their farewell addresses, both the Duke and Duchess used the French expression, au revoir, in their radio address to the nation, the majority of whose English-speaking native population would likely not even know the meaning of this phrase.

The Duke's public broadcast followed two farewell addresses to the governor on April 25, first by the president on behalf of the members of the Legislative Council, and secondly by the Speaker for members of the Honourable House of Assembly. His Excellency replied to both houses formally and identically with the following words:

> "I thank you for the Address you have presented to me on the eve of my departure from Nassau. During the almost five years of my Administration the Duchess and I have become greatly attached to The Bahamas, and we are gratified to know that our efforts on behalf of these Islands are appreciated by you. . . ."[88]

The royal governor was also given a parliamentary and official farewell dinner at the Bahamas Country Club on Friday, April 27. The event, as featured in the *Nassau Guardian* the next day, was reported to have enjoyed a large attendance of members of the legislature, the heads of all government departments, representatives of the armed forces, and included the Anglican bishop and the top American diplomat at the time. In all, 103 persons were present. The atmosphere was described as "cheerful good fellowship" and the food was said to be a "carefully composed menu befitting the occasion." There were three toasts: "The King," "His Royal Highness the Duke of Windsor," and "The Colony." Music was provided by the Royal Air Force band.[89]

---

88 Dupuch, "Report of Farewell Broadcast of Duke of Windsor."

89 "Farewell Dinner of Duke and Duchess of Windsor," *Nassau Guardian*,

On Sunday, April 29, the same day as their radio broadcast, the Duke and Duchess paid a farewell visit to the United States canteen, where a large number of men of the RAF and many of the canteen workers were present.

The Duchess was presented with a gift of a beautiful small silver tray with an inscription on behalf of the airmen who expressed the debt of gratitude that they owed to the Duchess for starting the canteen and for the deep interest she had always taken in it, and for her active work on behalf of the airmen. In fact many of the airmen referred to it as the "Duchess Canteen."

On April 30 there was a farewell gathering at the Infant Welfare Clinic on the Southern Recreation Grounds where many mothers with children gathered to express appreciation to the Duchess for all she had done for the local children. They gave the Duchess a polished turtle back as a gift, as well as presenting her with a beautiful bouquet of flowers. That evening, the Duke and Duchess hosted members of the Executive Council and all the heads of public departments and their wives to a farewell cocktail party on the terrace of Government House.

Two days later, on Wednesday, May 2, 1945, the Duke and Duchess departed The Bahamas and were en route to the United States.

After leaving The Bahamas the Duke did visit Nassau on two or three unofficial visits in later years, primarily to participate in golf tournaments. The Duchess never returned.

28 April 1945.

THE OFFICE

On July 28, 1945, Sir William L. Murphy, who had previously served as colonial secretary of Bermuda, was sworn in as governor and commander in chief of The Bahamas, successor in that office to the Duke of Windsor, who had departed in May.

Following him as royal governor of The Bahamas were seven appointments of English royal governors preceding Sir Milo B. Butler, who took office nearly thirty years later in 1973, the first Bahamian of colour to hold the high office of governor general in an independent Bahamas.

I was also privileged to have been appointed to this position by Her Majesty the Queen as her representative head of state of The Bahamas. As governor general, I received officials and dignitaries, both local and from foreign countries, who upon presenting their credentials were formally welcomed to The Bahamas as the official representatives of their respective countries. I was also privileged in my official capacity to likewise represent The Bahamas in visiting many foreign countries.

During the seven-year period that I occupied this official post I resided, together with my wife, Edith, at the historic governor general's residence on Mount Fitzwilliam. I had the honour of entertaining my family on these premises, being especially pleased to be able to witness the formative years of my grandchildren, including the youngest, who was born in March 1995, two months after I assumed office. The expansive grounds of Mount Fitzwilliam served as a wonderful playground for my grandchildren and their friends, all of whom have said they will always cherish their happy memories of this unique experience.

During my career in law, I had qualified both in The Bahamas as an attorney-at-law and in England as an English barrister-at-law, and practiced in The Bahamas for more than forty years at the time of my appointment as governor general. I had also served in several official posts in the government of The Bahamas, including as a member of the cabinet, where the laws are initiated; the office of the attorney general, where the laws are drafted; and the Parliament, where the laws are enacted. It was, therefore, a distinct honour as one of my official duties as governor general to be responsible for the final stage in the official enactment and promulgation of the law by signing the requisite legislative bills. I therefore had the rare privilege of serving in some capacity within each stage of the law.

When I assumed office as governor general, my mission was to devote my tenure to uplifting and motivating the schoolchildren of The Bahamas. Upon reflection, I think that my childhood living in Grant's Town just below Government House, to which I was prohibited from visiting in those days, impelled me to give all young Bahamians, whether black or white, the opportunity to experience what was then the rarity of visiting the highest and most prestigious official residence in our land.

To that end, in my capacity as governor general, I visited most of the schools in the country, including each one in New Providence and practically all in the Family Islands. During those trips, I invited all of the students to visit Government House and it was a great privilege and pleasure for me not only to receive diplomats and high officials but also to welcome the schoolchildren who came to see Government House.

I also made a point during my time in office to visit every Family Island in the The Bahamas, thereby helping to foster a sense of national unity and identity through the preservation of our institutions and traditions.

It has been my honour and privilege, and a great pleasure, to serve in such a high post in our country, and it is my hope that this boy from Over the Hill brought an openness of respect, dignity, and decorum to the People's House *On Top of the Hill!*

BIBLIOGRAPHY

Albury, P., *The Story of The Bahamas*, London & Basingstoke, Macmillan Press Ltd., 1975.

Allen, M., *Hidden Agenda,* London, Basingstoke & Oxford, Macmillan Publishers Ltd., 2000.

Bahamas Government, House of Assembly, Farewell Address of Duke of Windsor, 25 April 1945.

Bahamas Legislative Council, Farewell Address of Duke of Windsor, 25 April 1945.

Bahamas Government, The Statute Laws of The Bahamas: The Penal Code, Chapter 80/3.

Bethel, H. R., interviewed by Oral History team, College of The Bahamas, 1992.

Bethell, A. T., *The Early Settlers of The Bahamas*, Norfolk, Rounce & Wortley, 1937.

Bloch, M., *The Duchess of Windsor*, New York, St. Martin's Press, 1996.

Bocca, G., *The Life and Death of Sir Harry Oakes*, New York, Doubleday & Company, Inc., 1959.

Clifford, Sir B. to Ormsby-Gore, W., *Colonial Office Papers CO23/594/8*, Bahamas Department of Archives, 12 April 1937.

Clifford, Sir B. to Maffey, Sir John, *Colonial Office Papers CO23/580/8*, Bahamas Department of Archives, 13 January 1937.

Clifford, Sir B. to Maffey, Sir John, *Colonial Office Papers CO23/580/5*, Bahamas Department of Archives, 9 March 1937.

Cowan, B., *Sir Harry Oakes, 1874–1943: An Accumulation of Notes*, Cobalt, Ontario, Highway Book Shop, 2000.

Craton, M. and G. Saunders, *Islanders in the Stream*, vol. 1, Gainesville, University of Georgia Press, 1992.

Craton, M. and G. Saunders, *Islanders in the Stream*, vol. 2, Gainesville, University of Georgia Press, 1998.

Dupuch, E., Jr., *The Bahamas Handbook*, Nassau, Etienne Dupuch, Jr., Publications, 1961–1962.

Dupuch E., "Editorial: The Greatest Love Story of the Century," Nassau, *Nassau Daily Tribune*, 12 December 1936.

Dupuch, E., "Welcome to Duke and Duchess of Windsor," Nassau, *Nassau Daily Tribune*, 24 August 1940.

Dupuch, E., "Farewell Broadcast of Duke of Windsor," Nassau, *Nassau Daily Tribune*, 30 April 1945.

Fawkes R., *The Faith that Moved the Mountain*, Nassau, The Nassau Guardian, 1979.

Higham, C., *The Duchess of Windsor: The Secret Life*, New York, McGraw-Hill, 1988.

Houts, M., *King's X*, New York, William Morrow & Company, Inc., 1972.

Hughes, C. A., *Race and Politics in The Bahamas*, St. Lucia, University of Queensland Press, 1981.

Lawlor, A. & J., *The Harbour Island Story*, Oxford, MacMillan Education, 2008.

Leasor, J., *Who Killed Sir Harry Oakes?*, Boston, Houghton Mifflin Company, 1983.

Lloyd, T. K., Minute, *Colonial Office Papers CO23/785/7*, Bahamas Department of Archives, 30 May 1945.

Marigny, A. de', with M. Herskowitz, *A Conspiracy of Crowns*, New York, Crown Publishers Inc., 1990.

Martin, R. G., *The Woman He Loved*, New York, Simon and Schuster, 1974.

Miller, S., interviewed by Oral History team, College of The Bahamas, 1991; Thompson, Tracey L., "Remembering the Contract: Recollections of Bahamians," *The International Journal of Bahamian Studies,* accessed from http://journals.sfu.ca/cob/index.php/files/article/view/169/217, 18 June 2012.

Moss, J. M., "Tribute to Contract Workers." President of the
Bahamian American Association in 1993 addressed a special
lecture series at The College of The Bahamas, Nassau.

Pye, M., *The King Over the Water*, New York, Holt, Rinehart and
Winston, 1981.

Report, "Farewell Dinner of Duke and Duchess of Windsor," *Nassau
Guardian*, 28 April 1945.

Rolle, D., interviewed by Oral History team, College of The
Bahamas, 1991; Thompson, Tracey L., "Remembering the
Contract: Recollections of Bahamians," *The International Journal
of Bahamian Studies,* accessed from http://journals.sfu.ca/cob/
index.php/files/article/view/169/217, 18 June 2012.

Spoto, D., *The Decline and Fall of the House of Windsor*, New York,
Simon & Schuster, 1995.

Storr, Virgil H. and Nona Martin Storr, "I'se a Man," *Journal of
Caribbean History*, no. 41 (2008); conference paper, Society for
Caribbean Studies.

Thompson, A., *An Economic History of The Bahamas*, Nassau,
Commonwealth Publications Limited, 1979.

Williams, S., *The People's King*, London, Penguin Books Ltd., 2003.

Wilson, C., *Dancing with the Devil*, London, Harper Collins
Publishers, 2000.

Windsor, Wallis Warfield, Duchess of, *The Heart Has Its Reasons*,
London, The Companion Book Club, Odhams Press Ltd., 1958.

Windsor, Duke of, to Oliver Stanley, *Colonial Office Papers
CO23/967/126*, 8 March 1944.

Windsor, Duke of, to Sir John Stephens, *Colonial Office Papers
CO23/785*, 21 June 1945.

Zeigler, P., *King Edward VIII*, New York, Alfred A Kopf Inc., 1990.

Sir Orville Turnquest, GCMG, QC, LL.B., JP served as
governor general of The Bahamas from January 1995 until he
retired in November 2001.

In 1945 when the Duke of Windsor left The Bahamas, he was
followed by a succession of ten royal governors. After Bahamian
independence was declared on July 10, 1973, the name of the office
was changed from royal governor to governor general; Sir Orville
served in this high office as the fifth governor general.

He was born on July 19, 1929, the second son of Robert and
Gwendolyn Turnquest, and spent his early life in Grant's Town,
the urban residential area to the south of the city of Nassau, which
was inhabited by the underprivileged black community and
locally known as Over the Hill.

After completing his early education in The Bahamas, he
served as an articled law clerk to the late Honorable A. F.
Adderley, and successfully passed the local bar examination to
be admitted to The Bahamas bar. He practised for a few years
at the local bar and then travelled to London, where he successfully completed the English bar examinations; he also obtained his
LL.B. from London University, after which he was admitted to
the English bar as a member of Lincoln's Inn, London. Although
Sir Orville returned to Nassau where he successfully practised at
The Bahamas bar for many years, some years later he was elected

an honorary bencher of Lincoln's Inn, one of the revered institutions responsible for governing the legal profession in Britain and the colonies.

During a long and distinguished career as a practising lawyer in The Bahamas, in which he enjoyed a reputation as one of the country's leading litigants and public speakers, Sir Orville also served intermittently as a magistrate, as president of the Bahamas Bar Association, as lecturer in law at the Bahamas Extra-mural Department of the University of the West Indies, and as a member of the Law Revision Committee.

He has been on the political front line in The Bahamas for the greater part of his adult life, serving in both houses of Parliament almost continuously from 1962 until 1995 when he became governor general. During his political career, he served as chairman and later as deputy leader of his political party, the Free National Movement, and was also a delegate to the constitutional conferences in London in 1963 and 1972 leading up to Bahamian independence. Sir Orville has also served as attorney general, minister of justice, minister of foreign affairs, and deputy prime minister of The Bahamas.

Sir Orville resigned from active politics in November 1994, and on January 3, 1995, he was sworn in as governor general of the Commonwealth of The Bahamas in a colourful outdoor ceremony. Shortly afterwards he called on Her Majesty the Queen at Buckingham Palace in London, and was conferred with the accolade of Knight Grand Cross of the Order of St. Michael and St. George (GCMG).

During his tenure as governor general, Sir Orville welcomed scores of visitors and envoys from around the world at Government House in Nassau, and in turn travelled throughout the Family Islands of The Bahamas, as well as many cities across the United States, Central America, Brazil, Canada, Britain, most of the countries of Europe, Taiwan, China, Malta, Cyprus, East Africa, South Africa, and all the Caricom countries of the Caribbean region on missions of goodwill and the espousal of Bahamian friendship and mutual progress.

He has been the recipient of many honours over the years, including honorary doctorates from Elmira College, New York (1998), University of the West Indies (2000) and Sojourner-Douglass College, Maryland (2002). Other awards include membership in the President's Associates of Nova Southeastern University, Florida, and lifetime honorary membership in Rotary International, the Lions Club, 100 Black Men of America, the Scout Association of The Bahamas, the Salvation Army Advisory Board and other national, charitable, and civic organizations of The Bahamas.

In semiretirement, Sir Orville is in constant demand locally as a public speaker, serves as a consultant counsel to his former law firm, was a former lecturer at the Nassau Campus of Sojourner Douglass College, and now devotes a great deal of his time to historical research.

A devout and lifetime member of the Anglican Church in The Bahamas, he has served as chancellor of the Diocese of Nassau and The Bahamas, including the Turks and Caicos Islands, from 1962 until 2002.

Sir Orville feels privileged to have ascended to a highly esteemed office once held by the Duke of Windsor and is honoured to have ended his own political career as a successor to a former king of England.

CPSIA information can be obtained
at www.ICGtesting.com
Printed in the USA
FSOW01n1227181216
28729FS